# Instructor's Manual
## Chapters 18-26

# Accounting, 25e

## Carl S. Warren
*Professor Emeritus of Accounting*
*University of Georgia, Athens*

## James M. Reeve
*Professor Emeritus of Accounting*
*University of Tennessee, Knoxville*

## Jonathan E. Duchac
*Professor of Accounting*
*Wake Forest University*

SOUTH-WESTERN
CENGAGE Learning

Australia · Brazil · Japan · Korea · Mexico · Singapore · Spain · United Kingdom · United States

ISBN-13: 978-1-285-07854-0
ISBN-10: 1-285-07854-3

**South-Western Cengage Learning**
5191 Natorp Boulevard
Mason, OH 45040
USA

Cengage Learning is a leading provider of customized learning solutions with office locations around the globe, including Singapore, the United Kingdom, Australia, Mexico, Brazil, and Japan. Locate your local office at: **international.cengage.com/region**.

Cengage Learning products are represented in Canada by Nelson Education, Ltd.

For your course and learning solutions, visit **www.cengage.com**.

Purchase any of our products at your local college store or at our preferred online store **www.CengageBrain.com**.

Printed in the United States of America
1 2 3 4 5 6 7   17 16 15 14 13

# Contents

# Preface

The Instructor's Manual to accompany Warren/Reeve/Duchac's *Financial Accounting, 13th Edition,* and *Accounting, 25th edition,* has been thoroughly updated to reflect changes to the text and to provide the best ideas and resources for use in your course preparation and classroom presentation. The manual was revised by Kirk Lynch, Sandhills Community College.

## INSTRUCTOR'S MANUAL FEATURES

This manual contains a number of resources designed to aid instructors as they prepare lectures, assign homework, and teach in the classroom.

Key features (descriptions for several of these features are expanded below in the "Focus on Instructor's Resource Materials" section) include:

- A **List of Objectives** and **Brief Synopsis** for each chapter.

- **Student FAQs**, included near the beginning of every chapter, will be a valuable resource for beginning and seasoned professors alike. These lists of questions frequently asked in the classroom were compiled from suggestions from a panel of accounting professors.

- Exploration of each objective, including information on **Key Terms**, **Ideas for Class Discussion** and **Lecture Aids.**

- **Suggested Approaches** per objective, which incorporate many of the teaching initiatives being stressed in higher education today, including active learning, collaborative learning, critical thinking, and writing across the curriculum.

- **Demonstration problems** that can be used in the classroom to illustrate accounting practices. Working through an accounting problem gives the instructor an opportunity to point out pitfalls that students should avoid.

- **Group learning activities** that provide another opportunity to actively involve students in the learning process. These activities ask students to apply accounting topics by completing an assigned task in small groups of three to five students. Small group work is an excellent way to introduce variety into the accounting classroom and creates a more productive learning environment.

- **Writing exercises** that provide an opportunity for students to develop good written communication skills essential to any businessperson. These exercises probe students' knowledge of conceptual issues related to accounting.

- **Handouts** specifically designed for classroom use are included for select chapters. A full set of handout solutions are provided on the Instructor Resource DVD and the instructor's Web site.

- **Homework Charts with Learning Outcomes Tagging** have been added at the end of each chapter to show how Discussion Questions, Practice Exercises, and End-of-Chapter Exercises, Problems, and

Special Cases and Projects relate to the Key Learning Outcomes. Information provided for each assignment includes: level of difficulty, estimated completion time, and learning outcomes tagging for Business Program (formerly AACSB), AICPA, and IMA competencies. Bloom's Taxonomy outcomes have also been added. Assignments accompanied by spreadsheet templates and General Ledger software are designated. Abbreviations used in this chart are defined below:

DQ = Discussion Questions

PE = Practice Exercise

Ex = Exercise

Spreadsheet—indicates that the problem has an accompanying student spreadsheet template (available on the student companion Web site).

GL—indicates that the problem is also available in General Ledger software.

BUSPROG—Business Program (These outcome measures are equivalent to AACSB's.)

AICPA—learning outcomes established by the American Institute of Certified Public Accountants.

ACBSP—learning outcomes established by the Accreditation Council for Business Schools & Programs.

IMA—learning outcomes established by the Institute of Management Accountants.

Bloom's—indicates where the question fits under Bloom's Taxonomy.

Several items that appeared in past printed editions of the Instructor's Manual have been moved to another area. These include:

- The **Transparency Masters** (TMs) have been moved to the Instructor's Resource DVD and to the instructor's Web site.

- Information on using **General Ledger software and Inspector software** is available on the Instructor's Resource DVD.

# ADDITIONAL INSTRUCTOR RESOURCES

Beside the Instructor's Manual, there are a number of other Instructor Resources offered to help with your classroom management and preparation. These include:

**Solutions Manual:** The Solutions Manual contains answers to all exercises, problems, and activities that appear in the text. As always the solutions are author-written and verified multiple times for numerical accuracy and consistency with the core text.

**Test Bank:** For each chapter, the Test Bank includes True/False questions, Multiple-Choice questions, and Problems, each marked with a difficulty level, chapter objective association, and a tie-in to standard course outcomes. Along with the normal update and upgrade of the 2,800 test bank questions, variations of the Example Exercises have been added for further quizzing and better integration with the textbook.

In addition, the bank provides a grid for each chapter that compiles the correlation of each question to the individual chapter's objectives, as well as a ranking of difficulty based on a clearly described categorization. Through this helpful grid, making a test that is comprehensive and well-balanced is a snap!

**ExamView® Pro Testing Software:** This intuitive software allows you to easily customize exams, practice tests, and tutorials and deliver them over a network, on the Internet, or in printed form. In addition, ExamView comes with searching capabilities that make sorting the wealth of questions from the printed test bank easy. The software and files are found on the Instructor's Resource DVD (IR-DVD).

**PowerPoint®:** Each presentation, which is included on the Instructor's Resource DVD and on the product support site, enhances lectures and simplifies class preparation. Each chapter contains objectives followed by a thorough outline of the chapter that easily provide an entire lecture model. Also, exhibits from the chapter, such as the new Example Exercises, have been recreated as colorful PowerPoint slides to create a powerful, customizable tool.

**Instructor Excel® Templates:** These templates provide the solutions for the problems and exercises that have Enhanced Excel® templates for students. Through these files, instructors can see the solutions in the same format as the students. All problems with accompanying templates are marked in the book with an icon and are listed in the information grid in the solutions manual. These templates are available for download on academic.cengage.com/accounting/warren or on the Instructor's Resource DVD.

**Instructor's Resource DVD**: This convenient resource includes the PowerPoint® Presentations, Instructor's Manual, Solutions Manual, Test Bank, ExamView®, and Excel Template Solutions. All the basic material an instructor needs is available in one place.

**Product Support Web Site: login.cengage.com**
Our instructor Web site provides a variety of password-protected, instructor resources. You'll find text-specific and other related resources organized by chapter and topic. Many are also available on the Instructor's Resource DVD. To access the site, go to **login.cengage.com**, use your instructor sign-in credentials, and search for this title using the student ISBN on the back of your book. (First-time users can request login credentials at this site.)

# Supplement Materials in CengageNOW

Our supplement materials include many items that will help a student practice, study, and learn the concept presented in each chapter. These supplements are listed below. If you have adopted CengageNOW online homework solution for your course, your students have access to the following resources. The chart that follows this list identifies which assets are available with each chapter. Sources from the free student companion Web site are also included.

- **eBook:** Our eBook is linked from assigned homework (in CengageNOW) via the Personalized Student Plan (PSP) to the corresponding learning objective. This ancillary will return students to the originating content source; the materials as presented in the text.

- ◆ **eLecture:** Our eLecture PowerPoint decks are based on the main learning points presented in the chapter.

- ◆ **Animated Activities (NEW!):** Animated illustrations visually explain and guide students through selected core topics in introductory financial and managerial accounting. Each activity uses a realistic company example to illustrate how the concepts relate to the everyday activities of a business.

- ◆ **Activation Exercises (NEW!):** Author-created exercises that cover key terms, business transactions, recording into the accounting system, and how these are reflected in the financial statements.

- ◆ **Animated Example Exercise:** A PowerPoint deck utilizing both animation and voice-over have been created to step a student through each Example Exercise presented in each chapter.

- ◆ **Experience Accounting Videos:** See accounting come to life as accounting topics are placed in real business situations.

- ◆ **Quiz Bowl:** This quiz game is "Jeopardy!"-styled. Each game is organized by chapter and allows students to review key topics and an explanation of correct answer is provided!

- ◆ **Beat the Clock (NEW!):** Students can test their knowledge of accounting concepts with the goal of correctly answering as many questions as possible before the clock runs out.

- ◆ **Accounting Games:** Available for most chapters, students reinforce their understanding of key chapter concepts with fun, interactive games.

- ◆ **Crossword Puzzle:** Drawn from the glossary, laid out by chapter, these interactive puzzles provide an additional tool for students to test their understanding of accounting terminology.

- ◆ **Flashcards:** Drawn from the glossary, laid out by chapter, the flashcards aid student's learning through repetition of key concepts and their definitions.

See the chart on the following page for which resources appear with each chapter.

| Chapter | Available in CengageNOW | | | | | | | | Also available on the Student companion Web site | |
|---|---|---|---|---|---|---|---|---|---|---|
| | eBook | eLecture | Animated Example Exercise | Experience Accounting Videos | Quiz Bowl | Accounting Games | Animated Activities | Activation Exercises | Crossword Puzzle | Flashcards |
| 1 Introduction to Accounting and Business | ✓ | ✓ | ✓ | | ✓ | | | | ✓ | ✓ |
| 2 Analyzing Transactions | ✓ | ✓ | ✓ | | ✓ | ✓ | ✓ | ✓ | ✓ | ✓ |
| 3 The Adjusting Process | ✓ | ✓ | ✓ | | ✓ | ✓ | | ✓ | ✓ | ✓ |
| 4 Completing the Accounting Cycle | ✓ | ✓ | ✓ | | ✓ | | | ✓ | ✓ | ✓ |
| 5 Accounting Systems | ✓ | ✓ | ✓ | | ✓ | ✓ | ✓ | ✓ | ✓ | ✓ |
| 6 Accounting for Merchandising Businesses | ✓ | ✓ | ✓ | | ✓ | ✓ | ✓ | ✓ | ✓ | ✓ |
| 7 Inventories | ✓ | ✓ | ✓ | | ✓ | | ✓ | | ✓ | ✓ |
| 8 Sarbanes-Oxley, Internal Control and Cash | ✓ | ✓ | ✓ | | ✓ | | | | ✓ | ✓ |
| 9 Receivables | ✓ | ✓ | ✓ | | ✓ | ✓ | ✓ | ✓ | ✓ | ✓ |

| Chapter | Available in CengageNOW | | | | | | | | Also available on the Student companion Web site | |
|---|---|---|---|---|---|---|---|---|---|---|
| | eBook | eLecture | Animated Example Exercise | Experience Accounting Videos | Quiz Bowl | Accounting Games | Animated Activities | Activation Exercises | Crossword Puzzle | Flashcards |
| 10 Fixed Assets and Intangible Assets | ✓ | ✓ | ✓ | | ✓ | ✓ | ✓ | ✓ | ✓ | ✓ |
| 11 Current Liabilities and Payroll | ✓ | ✓ | ✓ | | ✓ | ✓ | | ✓ | ✓ | ✓ |
| 12 Accounting for Partnerships and Limited Liability Companies | ✓ | ✓ | ✓ | | ✓ | | | ✓ | ✓ | ✓ |
| 13 Corporations: Organization, Stock Transactions, and Dividends | ✓ | ✓ | ✓ | | ✓ | ✓ | ✓ | ✓ | ✓ | ✓ |
| 14 Long-term Liabilities: Bonds & Notes | ✓ | ✓ | ✓ | | ✓ | ✓ | ✓ | ✓ | ✓ | ✓ |
| 15 Investments and Fair Value Accounting | ✓ | ✓ | ✓ | | ✓ | ✓ | | | ✓ | ✓ |
| 16 Statement of Cash Flows | ✓ | ✓ | ✓ | | ✓ | ✓ | | | ✓ | ✓ |
| 17 Financial Statement Analysis | ✓ | ✓ | ✓ | | ✓ | ✓ | | | ✓ | ✓ |

| Chapter | Available in CengageNOW | | | | | | | | Also available on the Student companion Web site | |
|---|---|---|---|---|---|---|---|---|---|---|
| | eBook | eLecture | Animated Example Exercise | Experience Accounting Videos | Quiz Bowl | Accounting Games | Animated Activities | Activation Exercises | Crossword Puzzle | Flashcards |
| 18 Managerial Accounting Concepts and Principles | ✓ | | | | | | | | | |
| 19 Job Order Costing | ✓ | ✓ | ✓ | ✓ | ✓ | ✓ | ✓ | | ✓ | ✓ |
| 20 Process Cost Systems | ✓ | ✓ | ✓ | ✓ | ✓ | ✓ | | | ✓ | ✓ |
| 21 Cost Behavior & Cost-Volume-Profit Analysis | ✓ | ✓ | ✓ | ✓ | ✓ | ✓ | ✓ | | ✓ | ✓ |
| 22 Budgeting | ✓ | ✓ | ✓ | ✓ | ✓ | ✓ | ✓ | | ✓ | ✓ |
| 23 Performance Evaluation Using Variances from Standard Costs | ✓ | ✓ | ✓ | | ✓ | ✓ | | | ✓ | ✓ |
| 24 Performance Evaluation for Decentralized Operations | ✓ | ✓ | ✓ | | ✓ | ✓ | | | ✓ | ✓ |

| Chapter | Available in CengageNOW | | | | | | | | Also available on the Student companion Web site | |
|---|---|---|---|---|---|---|---|---|---|---|
| | eBook | eLecture | Animated Example Exercise | Experience Accounting Videos | Quiz Bowl | Accounting Games | Animated Activities | Activation Exercises | Crossword Puzzle | Flashcards |
| 25 Differential Analysis, Product Pricing, and Activity-Based Costing | ✓ | ✓ | ✓ | | ✓ | ✓ | ✓ | | ✓ | ✓ |
| 26 Capital Investment Analysis | ✓ | ✓ | ✓ | ✓ | ✓ | ✓ | ✓ | | ✓ | ✓ |

# Focus on Instructor's Resource Materials

The Instructor's Resource Materials are designed to provide you with fresh ideas for teaching accounting. These materials should minimize your classroom preparation time by providing lecture aids and practical teaching suggestions that are easy to carry directly into the classroom.

The teaching suggestions emulate many of the teaching initiatives being stressed in higher education today, including active learning, collaborative learning, critical thinking, and writing across the curriculum. These initiatives are integrated into the PowerPoint lecture notes, demonstration problems, group learning activities, and writing exercises that accompany each chapter. The following notes will assist you in using these features effectively in your classes.

## DEMONSTRATION PROBLEMS

You can use the demonstration problems to illustrate accounting practices. Most students like to see accounting methods demonstrated in the classroom prior to attempting homework problems. This gives the instructor a chance to point out pitfalls to avoid and provides an opportunity to stress underlying concepts and practical applications. Demonstration problems can be presented by using the traditional lecture mode of instruction. However, with only slight modifications in teaching style, they can be used to move students from passive note takers to active learners.

Rather than working through an entire problem for students, ask them to perform simple steps or calculations on their own. For example, assume you are working a problem in class that illustrates the process of recording business transactions. Complete a few entries for your students and then instruct them to record the next entry on their own. After giving them a minute to think and record their answer, present the correct solution. This forces students into an active role and gives them immediate feedback.

Consider asking students to perform all formula-based calculations that accompany demonstration problems. For example, give students the formula to calculate straight-line depreciation and the data to be applied, and then ask them to calculate the answer. This forces students to match the raw data with a formula. As students become more comfortable with performing calculations in class, you can work to wean them from a formula-based approach to accounting in favor of a conceptual-based approach. For example, rather than showing your students a formula to calculate straight-line depreciation, describe the concept, present example data, and ask them to decipher the calculation.

## GROUP LEARNING ACTIVITIES

Group learning activities provide another way to actively involve students. They must complete assigned tasks in small groups of three to five, involving them in collaborative learning by asking questions and helping each other master course content. Small group work is an excellent way to introduce variety into the classroom. It also encourages questions, since many students are more comfortable with admitting what they don't know in a small group than in front of the entire class. Group work allows students to discover solutions, rather than being shown a solution. It also frees the instructor to move through the class and work with the groups.

Group learning activities may be more productive if you do not allow students to choose their own groups. When students do so, they usually work with friends or students with similar academic abilities. Groups provide the best learning environment if top students are mixed with average and poor students. You may want to assign groups randomly at the beginning of the term. After the first test results are in, you can reassign groups so that each contains a student who excelled on the first exam, as well as students who earned average and poor grades.

One easy way to break the class into groups is to distribute cards. At the beginning of the term, ask each student to pick one card from a deck of playing cards. Ask students to form groups of four, based on the card they choose (all kings are a group, etc.). Cards also make it easy to assign roles to individual group members. For example, you can assign the following roles for each activity:

1. Leader—makes sure that the task is completed in the allocated time.
2. Reporter—records and reports results to the class.
3. Socializer—makes sure that all group members are involved in the assignment. For example, if one member is not participating, the socializer should make it a point to ask for his or her input.
4. E.P.A. (Environmental Protection Agent)—makes sure that all desks and chairs are back in the proper place at the end of the activity.

By distributing the playing cards, you assign these roles by choosing a suit (e.g., the leader will be the spade, the reporter will be the heart). The cards also give you the flexibility to rotate roles daily

## WRITING EXERCISES

Good written communication skills are essential to any businessperson. The textbook includes writing exercises designed to help students sharpen their communication skills. This Instructor's Manual also includes writing exercises. However, these exercises concentrate on writing as a learning tool, rather than writing as a means to a finished document. If students can express a concept in writing, they understand that concept. Both you and the students can determine exactly what they do and do not understand. Writing can make students vividly aware of gaps in their knowledge.

The writing assignments will ask students to respond to specific questions that probe their knowledge of conceptual issues related to accounting. They are designed to be completed in one to three minutes. As the instructor, you have several options on how to use these writing exercises. You may want to collect your students' responses to gauge how well the class is grasping the course material. By reading even a sample from the responses, you can usually assess students' overall understanding of the material.

As an alternative, you could ask students to share their responses in small groups. This allows students who do understand course material to share their ideas with students who are struggling with concepts.

# Managerial Accounting Concepts and Principles

## OPENING COMMENTS

Chapter 18 introduces students to managerial accounting and the manufacturing process. Students will learn how managerial accounting is used in the management decision process. They will also be exposed to the terminology used to describe costs related to manufacturing.

Students learn how costs flow through a manufacturing system.

After studying the chapter, your students should be able to:

1.  Describe managerial accounting and the role of managerial accounting in a business.

2.  Define and illustrate the following costs: 1. direct and indirect costs, 2. direct materials, direct labor, and factory overhead costs, 3. product and period costs.

3.  Describe and illustrate the following statements for a manufacturing business: 1. balance sheet, 2. statement of cost of goods manufactured, 3. income statement.

4.  Describe the uses of managerial accounting information.

## STUDENT FAQS

*   Why is conversion cost considered to be direct labor and factory overhead?

*   Why is direct and indirect cost so important to understand?

*   Why is product and period cost so important to understand?

*   Why do we have to maintain all these costs for each specific job?

*   Why is direct labor both a prime and a conversion cost? Isn't that double accounting?

# OBJECTIVE 1

Describe managerial accounting and the role of managerial accounting in a business.

## KEY TERMS

Continuous Process Improvement
Controller
Controlling
Decision Making
Directing
Feedback
Financial Accounting
Line Department
Management by Exception

Management Process
Managerial Accounting
Objectives (goals)
Operational Planning
Planning
Staff Department
Strategic Planning
Strategies

## SUGGESTED APPROACH — Differences in Financial and Managerial Accounting

Use Transparency Master (TM) 18-1 to review the basic differences between financial and managerial accounting. It is helpful to point out that financial accounting stresses stewardship of assets (a historical orientation), while managerial accounting stresses the best alternative uses of assets (a future orientation).

## CLASS DISCUSSION — Managerial Accounting Reports

Ask students whether they receive or prepare any financial reports in their jobs, other than the financial accounting reports discussed in previous chapters. Ask them to describe these reports and comment on how management uses them to run the business.

## WRITING EXERCISE — Managerial Accounting

Instruct your students to write an answer to the following question (TM 18-2):

Why is it permissible to violate generally accepted accounting principles when preparing reports used strictly by company management?

**Possible response**: Since these reports are for internal use only, they should not provide any influence to investors about decisions to invest in the company. These reports are for management to aid in the decision making process. It should be clear to all users that these reports may not follow GAAP.

## CLASS DISCUSSION — Management Accountants

The role of the management accountant is to provide management with information needed to plan and control the operations of a business. The Group Learning Activity below will ask your students to assume the role of a manager in a variety of business situations. In this role, they must request information from their company's management accounting department to assist them in their management functions. This exercise allows students to experience how management accountants participate in the management process.

This section also introduces your students to the controller's position in the typical organizational chart. This is an opportune time to expose students to the Certificate in Management Accounting (CMA) program. TM 18-3 outlines the requirements for obtaining this credential. The following website is also helpful in determining the CMA requirements: http://www.imanet.org/index.asp.

## GROUP LEARNING ACTIVITY — Managerial Accounting in the Management Process

Divide the class into small groups. Handouts 18-1 through 18-5 each presents a manager who needs information that can be supplied by managerial accounting. Assign each of the groups one of these scenarios. Ask them to read the scenario and list the information that the manager should request from the management accounting department.

**Possible responses:**

**Handout 8-1:** One possible explanation is a recent change in supplier. If this is the case, the accounting department can supply cost per yard of material from old supplier verses new supplier. They can then factor in the increased scrap cost to determine if overall costs are more or less than the previous supplier. It could be that the new supplier is cheaper per yard up front, but increased scrap cost results in overall higher cost.

**Handout 8-2:** Credit cards and ATM cards come with a processing fee that cash does not require. This additional expense will cut into the bottom line. However, increased cost might be overcome with increased sales to customers who will spend more with the convenience of shopping with a card. Accounting can provide an analysis of processing fees to determine the level to which sales must increase in order to break even.

**Handout 8-3:** As the new sales manager focusing on Buddy at this time, I would want to know the following information for the company and for each sales representative individually:

> Total sales
> Sales returns
> Uncollectable accounts
> Selling expenses

Focusing on uncollectable accounts, sales returns as a percentage of total sales, I would want to examine if Buddy's numbers are significantly different from the company and how these ratios look compared to other high performing sales reps.

**Handout 8-4:** The manager will need to know what costs are included in the overhead reporting. Additionally, it would be beneficial to have historical data on these costs, as well as production numbers for these same time periods. It would also be beneficial to have sales projections for the quarter in question to match demand with cost.

**Handout 8-5:** The manager will need to know what materials go into the manufacturing process, the average amount used in each unit, the average cost for direct materials, the average time to manufacture the product, average wages for direct labor in the manufacturing process, projected sales for the period, and the desired ending inventory of finished goods, as well as current finished goods inventory. These will be a good starting point for discussion of the manufacturing process.

## GROUP LEARNING ACTIVITY — Organizational Chart

Ask your students to work in groups to construct an organizational chart for your college. You may want to give them a list of major departments/divisions within the organization. Once the chart is complete, instruct students to identify staff and line functions.

## SUGGESTED APPROACH — Management Process

Cover the five basic phases of the management process:
a.   Planning—used by management to develop the organization's objectives (goals) and to translate these objectives into courses of action.
1.   Strategic planning—long-term courses of action to achieve goals usually in five to ten years
2.   Operational planning—short-term courses of action.
b.   Directing—the process by which managers run day-to-day operations.
c.   Controlling—consists of monitoring the operating results of implemented plans and comparing the actual results with the expected results.
d.   Improving—uses process information to eliminate the *source* of problems in a process, so that the process delivers the right products (services) in the right quantities at the right time.
e.   Decision making—part of each of the four management processes above, developing a future plan to respond to unfavorable performances.

## INTERNET ACTIVITY — Resources for Management Accountants

Direct your students to visit the Institute of Management Accountants' (IMA) Web site at http://www.imanet.org/index.asp. The IMA is the professional organization supporting management accountants. To familiarize students with the resources available to management accountants through the IMA, instruct your students to print out one or more of the following: the IMA's mission, information on the IMA Ethics Center, the IMA's Statement of Ethical Professional Practice, or information on the CMA certification.

# OBJECTIVE 2

Describe and illustrate the following costs: 1. direct and indirect costs, 2. direct materials, direct labor, and factory overhead costs, 3. product and period costs.

## KEY TERMS

| | |
|---|---|
| Conversion Costs | Factory Overhead Cost |
| Cost | Indirect Costs |
| Cost Object | Manufacturing Overhead |
| Direct Costs | Period Costs |
| Direct Labor Cost | Prime Costs |
| Direct Materials Cost | Product Costs |
| Factory Burden | |

## SUGGESTED APPROACH

Begin by contrasting merchandising and manufacturing operations. Remind students that merchandisers purchase a product and sell it. Manufacturers purchase parts and raw materials, make a product, and sell it. You may want to ask your students to list examples of service, merchandising, and manufacturing companies.

TMs 18-4 and 18-5 provide information to assist you in reviewing the major categories of manufacturing costs: direct materials, direct labor, and factory overhead. After explaining these categories, check your students' understanding by asking them to complete the writing exercise below.

## WRITING EXERCISE — Manufacturing Costs

Ask your students to write the headings of two large columns: title the first column "Product Costs" and the second column "Period Costs." Under the "Product Costs" column, divide into three subheadings, naming them Direct Materials, Direct Labor, and Factory Overhead. "Period Cost" can be divided into two subheadings of Administrative Cost and Selling Cost. Point out an item in the classroom (such as a chair, table, or textbook) and instruct students to list the costs necessary to manufacture the item. These costs should be listed under the appropriate heading.

## LECTURE AID — Period Costs

Objective 2 also introduces the term "period costs." These costs are selling and administrative expenses. TM 18-6 adds these costs to the diagram previously shown on TM 18-5.

## GROUP LEARNING ACTIVITY — Concepts and Terminology

Divide the class into groups of three with one in the middle as a recorder. Give two minutes of working time on each exercise. You must push them to get them to work each in two minutes. This is important so they learn that they must know how to classify these costs very quickly. Work each of the exercises 18-1 through 18-8 at the end of Chapter 18 in the textbook.

Use the Instructor's Resource CD to show correct answers as you progress quickly through these. Again, stress to the students at the end that they must know how to classify these costs or they will miss many answers in the future.

# OBJECTIVE 3

**Describe and illustrate the following statements for a manufacturing business: 1. balance sheet, 2. statement of cost of goods manufactured, 3. income statement.**

## KEY TERMS

Cost of Finished Goods Available

Cost of Goods Manufactured

Cost of Goods Sold

Cost of Merchandise Sold

Finished Goods Inventory

Materials Inventory

Merchandise Available for Sale

Statement of Cost of Goods Manufactured

Work in Process Inventory

## SUGGESTED APPROACH

Contrast a merchandising and manufacturing business. Use your local gas station as a merchandising business. It buys and then sells students gasoline without doing anything to the product. This type of business will have one type of inventory—gasoline, if they do not sell anything else. For a manufacturing business, use something such as the local sub/sandwich shop at your school; they manufacture or produce different sandwiches from different meats, cheeses, vegetables, and spreads. They start with the direct materials just discussed, add direct labor to make the sandwiches, and toss in some cost for the use of the equipment, building, heat, air conditioner, the oven, the cash register, the indirect labor of the cash register person, etc. You may even make and bake cookies to demonstrate a manufacturing business as a bakery business. You can illustrate beginning inventory, work in process inventory, and finished goods inventory (if you hurry before they eat the cookies) by stopping at various points. This takes a lot of preparation ahead of time.

The income statement is the first statement that needs preparation in any type of business; so it is with a manufacturing-type business. Cost of merchandise sold for a merchandising business is figured as shown below:

Beginning inventory

+ Purchases

= Merchandise available for sale

− Ending inventory

= Cost of merchandise sold

Cost of goods sold is calculated differently for a manufacturing company, due to the flow of costs through three different inventory accounts: raw materials, work in process, and finished goods.

The statement of cost of goods manufactured shows the flow of costs into and out of raw materials inventory, then the flow of costs into work in process, and the work in process inventory into finished goods inventory. (See TM 18-7.)

The calculations involved are:

Beginning Inventory—Raw Materials
+ Net Purchases
= Total Raw Materials Available for Use
− Ending Inventory—Raw Materials
= Raw Materials Placed in Production

Beginning Work in Process
+ Raw Materials Placed in Production
+ Labor Charged to Work in Process
+ Overhead Charged to Work in Process
− Ending Work In Process
= Cost of Goods Manufactured

The income statement shows the flow of finished goods inventory into the cost of goods sold. (See TM 18-8.)

The calculations are:

Beginning Finished Goods Inventory
+ Cost of Goods Manufactured
= Cost of Finished Goods Available for Sale
− Ending Finished Goods Inventory
= Cost of Goods Sold

# OBJECTIVE 4

Describe the uses of managerial accounting information.

## SUGGESTED APPROACH

Use the related Cases & Projects as a basis for class discussion.

The uses of managerial accounting reports are limited only by the imagination of the managers who use them. Some managers want endless details to analyze while others want a few summary items to review. The managerial accounting reports should reflect the needs and styles of the business. The text provides a few possible managerial uses of accounting information for the guitar manufacturing business discussed. These can be used as a starting point to generate discussion of other manufacturing businesses that your students may suggest or be interested in discussing.

# Managerial Accounting Scenario 1

The manager of a fabric store has noticed a considerable increase in the amount of defective fabric being scrapped by his store. Clerks notice the defects (such as irregularities in the weave or color of fabric) when they cut yardage from bolts of fabric. These defects usually affect only a small portion of the fabric on a bolt. Therefore, when a clerk discovers a defect, the "bad spot" is cut from the bolt. The clerk fills out a defect slip, which includes the amount of defective fabric (in yards), the retail price per yard, and the inventory control number. The defect slip is attached to the fabric and put in a "defects" bin in the storeroom. Once a month, the assistant manager sends the defect slips to the accounting department and packages the bad fabric for sale as scrap material. The accounting department uses the defect slips to write off the defective inventory in the accounting records.

What information could the manager request from the management accounting department that might help in attacking the problem of increasing defects?

# Managerial Accounting Scenario 2

The top management of a fast-food hamburger chain is considering installing point-of-sale machines that will allow customers to pay for food with an automated teller-machine card. Previously, the restaurant has accepted only cash.

What information could the management accounting department supply to assist management with this decision?

# Managerial Accounting Scenario 3

B Squared Inc. manufactures and sells awnings all over the southeastern United States. Each state has a sales representative who is paid on commissions. Each salesperson is responsible for checking the credit of customers as part of the sales process. Buddy has been the top salesman for the past 5 years in a row. You have been hired as the new sales manager and after meeting with your sales representatives, there are some questions being raised as to why Buddy is the top salesperson and the legitimacy of some of the sales being reported. What information would you request from the accounting department to help confirm or negate these accusations?

# Managerial Accounting Scenario 4

You are the newly hired production manager for the XYZ Company manufacturing plant and have been ask by the VP of manufacturing to provide a budget for the next quarter production for overhead cost.  What information will you need from accounting to assist in building this report?

# Managerial Accounting Scenario 5

You are the newly hired production manager for the XYZ Company manufacturing plant and have been ask by the VP of manufacturing to provide a budget for the next quarter production for prime cost. What information will you need from accounting to assist in building this report?

# HOMEWORK CHART WITH LEARNING OUTCOMES TAGGING

| Problem | Learning Objective | Description | DIFFICULTY | BUSPROG Primary | ACBSP Primary | ACBSP Secondary | IMA Managerial Only | BLOOM'S | TIME | Spread-sheet | GL |
|---|---|---|---|---|---|---|---|---|---|---|---|
| DQ18-1 | 18-1 | | Easy | Analytic | Managerial Characteristics/Terminology | | Cost Management | Knowledge | 5 min. | | |
| DQ18-2 | 18-1 | | Easy | Analytic | Managerial Characteristics/Terminology | | Cost Management | Knowledge | 5 min. | | |
| DQ18-3 | 18-2 | | Easy | Analytic | Managerial Accounting Features/Costs | | Cost Management | Knowledge | 5 min. | | |
| DQ18-4 | 18-2 | | Easy | Analytic | Managerial Accounting Features/Costs | | Cost Management | Knowledge | 5 min. | | |
| DQ18-5 | 18-2 | | Easy | Analytic | Managerial Accounting Features/Costs | | Cost Management | Knowledge | 5 min. | | |
| DQ18-6 | 18-3 | | Easy | Analytic | Managerial Accounting Features/Costs | | Cost Management | Knowledge | 5 min. | | |
| DQ18-7 | 18-3 | | Easy | Analytic | Managerial Accounting Features/Costs | | Cost Management | Knowledge | 5 min. | | |
| DQ18-8 | 18-3 | | Easy | Analytic | Managerial Accounting Features/Costs | | Cost Management | Knowledge | 5 min. | | |
| DQ18-9 | 18-3 | | Easy | Analytic | Managerial Accounting Features/Costs | | Cost Management | Knowledge | 5 min. | | |
| DQ18-10 | 18-3 | | Easy | Analytic | Managerial Accounting Features/Costs | | Cost Management | Knowledge | 5 min. | | |
| PE18-1A | 18-1 | Management process | Easy | Analytic | Management Functions | | Cost Management | Knowledge | 5 min. | | |
| PE18-1B | 18-1 | Management process | Easy | Analytic | Management Functions | | Cost Management | Knowledge | 5 min. | | |
| PE18-2A | 18-2 | Direct materials, direct labor, and factory overhead | Easy | Analytic | Managerial Accounting Features/Costs | | Cost Management | Knowledge | 5 min. | | |
| PE18-2B | 18-2 | Direct materials, direct labor, and factory overhead | Easy | Analytic | Managerial Accounting Features/Costs | | Cost Management | Knowledge | 5 min. | | |

| Problem | Learning Objective | Description | DIFFICULTY | BUSPROG Primary | ACBSP Primary | ACBSP Secondary | IMA Managerial Only | BLOOM'S | TIME | Spread-sheet | GL |
|---------|-------------------|-------------|------------|-----------------|---------------|-----------------|---------------------|---------|------|-------------|-----|
| PE18-3A | 18-2 | Prime and conversion costs | Easy | Analytic | Managerial Accounting Features/Costs | | Cost Management | Knowledge | 5 min. | | |
| PE18-3B | 18-2 | Prime and conversion costs | Easy | Analytic | Managerial Accounting Features/Costs | | Cost Management | Knowledge | 5 min. | | |
| PE18-4A | 18-2 | Product and period costs | Easy | Analytic | Managerial Accounting Features/Costs | | Cost Management | Knowledge | 5 min. | | |
| PE18-4B | 18-2 | Product and period costs | Easy | Analytic | Managerial Accounting Features/Costs | | Cost Management | Knowledge | 5 min. | | |
| PE18-5A | 18-3 | Cost of goods sold, cost of goods manufactured | Easy | Analytic | Managerial Accounting Features/Costs | | Cost Management | Application | 10 min. | | |
| PE18-5B | 18-3 | Cost of goods sold, cost of goods manufactured | Easy | Analytic | Managerial Accounting Features/Costs | | Cost Management | Application | 10 min. | | |
| Ex18-1 | 18-2 | Classifying costs as materials, labor, or factory overhead | Easy | Analytic | Managerial Accounting Features/Costs | | Cost Management | Knowledge | 10 min. | | |
| Ex18-2 | 18-2 | Classifying costs as materials, labor, or factory overhead | Easy | Analytic | Managerial Accounting Features/Costs | | Cost Management | Knowledge | 10 min. | | |
| Ex18-3 | 18-2 | Classifying costs as factory overhead | Easy | Analytic | Managerial Accounting Features/Costs | | Cost Management | Knowledge | 10 min. | | |
| Ex18-4 | 18-2 | Classifying costs as product or period costs | Easy | Analytic | Managerial Accounting Features/Costs | | Cost Management | Knowledge | 10 min. | | |
| Ex18-5 | 18-1, 18-2 | Concepts and terminology | Easy | Analytic | Managerial Characteristics/Terminology | | Cost Management | Knowledge | 5 min. | | |
| Ex18-6 | 18-1, 18-2 | Concepts and terminology | Easy | Analytic | Managerial Characteristics/Terminology | | Cost Management | Knowledge | 5 min. | | |
| Ex18-7 | 18-2 | Classifying costs in a service company | Easy | Analytic | Managerial Accounting Features/Costs | | Cost Management | Knowledge | 10 min. | | |
| Ex18-8 | 18-3 | Classifying costs | Moderate | Analytic | Managerial Accounting Features/Costs | | Cost Management | Application | 15 min. | | |
| Ex18-9 | 18-3 | Financial statements of a manufacturing firm | Moderate | Analytic | Financial Statements | | Cost Management | Application | 30 min. | | |

| Problem | Learning Objective | Description | DIFFICULTY | BUSPROG Primary | ACBSP Primary | ACBSP Secondary | IMA Managerial Only | BLOOM'S | TIME | Spreadsheet | GL |
|---|---|---|---|---|---|---|---|---|---|---|---|
| Ex18-10 | 18-3 | Manufacturing company balance sheet | Easy | Analytic | Current Assets | | Cost Management | Application | 10 min. | | |
| Ex18-11 | 18-3 | Cost of direct materials used in production for a manufacturing company | Easy | Analytic | Managerial Accounting Features/Costs | | Cost Management | Application | 10 min. | | |
| Ex18-12 | 18-3 | Cost of goods manufactured for a manufacturing company | Easy | Analytic | Managerial Accounting Features/Costs | | Cost Management | Application | 10 min. | | |
| Ex18-13 | 18-3 | Cost of goods manufactured for a manufacturing company | Easy | Analytic | Managerial Accounting Features/Costs | | Cost Management | Application | 10 min. | | |
| Ex18-14 | 18-3 | Income statement for a manufacturing company | Easy | Analytic | Financial Statements | | Cost Management | Application | 10 min. | | |
| Ex18-15 | 18-3 | Statement of cost of goods manufactured for a manufacturing company | Moderate | Analytic | Financial Statements | | Cost Management | Application | 30 min. | X | |
| Ex18-16 | 18-3 | and net income for a manufacturing | Moderate | Analytic | Financial Statements | | Management | Application | 15 min. | | |
| Ex18-17 | 18-3 | Cost flow relationships | Moderate | Analytic | Managerial Accounting Features/Costs | | Cost Management | Application | 30 min. | | |
| Pr18-1A | 18-2 | Classifying costs | Moderate | Analytic | Managerial Accounting Features/Costs | | Cost Management | Knowledge | 45 min. | | |
| Pr18-2A | 18-2 | Classifying costs | Moderate | Analytic | Managerial Accounting Features/Costs | | Cost Management | Knowledge | 45 min. | | |
| Pr18-3A | 18-2 | Cost classifications-service company | Moderate | Analytic | Managerial Accounting Features/Costs | | Cost Management | Knowledge | 45 min. | | |
| Pr18-4A | 18-2, 18-3 | Manufacturing income statement, statement of cost of goods manufactured | Challenging | Analytic | Managerial Accounting Features/Costs | Financial Statements | Cost Management | Application | 1.5 hours | X | |
| Pr18-5A | 18-2, 18-3 | Statement of cost of goods manufactured and income statement for a manufacturing company | Challenging | Analytic | Managerial Accounting Features/Costs | Financial Statements | Cost Management | Application | 1 hour | X | |
| Pr18-1B | 18-2 | Classifying costs | Moderate | Analytic | Managerial Accounting Features/Costs | | Cost Management | Knowledge | 45 min. | | |
| Pr18-2B | 18-2 | Classifying costs | Moderate | Analytic | Managerial Accounting Features/Costs | | Cost Management | Knowledge | 45 min. | | |

| Problem | Learning Objective | Description | DIFFICULTY | BUSPROG Primary | ACBSP Primary | ACBSP Secondary | IMA Managerial Only | BLOOM'S | TIME | Spreadsheet | GL |
|---|---|---|---|---|---|---|---|---|---|---|---|
| Pr18-3B | 18-2 | Cost classifications-service company | Moderate | Analytic | Managerial Accounting Features/Costs | | Cost Management | Knowledge | 45 min. | | |
| Pr18-4B | 18-2, 18-3 | Manufacturing income statement, statement of cost of goods manufactured | Challenging | Analytic | Managerial Accounting Features/Costs | | Cost Management | Application | 1.5 hours | X | |
| Pr18-5B | 18-2, 18-3 | Statement of cost of goods manufactured and income statement for a manufacturing company | Challenging | Analytic | Managerial Accounting Features/Costs | | Cost Management | Application | 1 hour | X | |
| CP18-1 | 18-1 | Ethics and professional conduct in business | Easy | Ethics | Managerial Accounting Features/Costs | | Cost Management | Analysis | 15 min. | | |
| CP18-2 | 18-1 | Financial vs. managerial accounting | Easy | Analytic | Managerial Characteristics/Terminology | | Cost Management | Analysis | 15 min. | | |
| CP18-3 | 18-1 | Managerial accounting in the management process | Easy | Analytic | Managerial Characteristics/Terminology | | Cost Management | Comprehension | 15 min. | | |
| CP18-4 | 18-2 | Classifying costs | Moderate | Analytic | Managerial Characteristics/Terminology | | Cost Management | Application | 1 hour | | |
| CP18-5 | 18-4 | Using managerial accounting information | Easy | Analytic | Management Functions | | Cost Management | Application | 30 min. | | |
| CP18-6 | 18-2 | Classifying costs | Moderate | Analytic | Managerial Accounting Features/Costs | | Cost Management | Application | 2 hours | | |

# Job Order Costing

## OPENING COMMENTS

Chapter 19 introduces students to managerial job order cost systems. Students will be exposed to the terminology used to describe costs related to manufacturing.

The first of two basic manufacturing accounting systems, job order, is described in this chapter. Students learn how costs flow through a manufacturing system and the basis for determining product costs under job order costing.

After studying the chapter, your students should be able to:

1. Describe cost accounting systems used by manufacturing businesses.

2. Describe and illustrate a job order cost accounting system.

3. Describe the use of job order cost information for decision making.

4. Describe the flow of costs for a service business that uses a job order cost accounting system.

## STUDENT FAQS

- Why is it necessary to calculate a predetermined overhead rate?

- Why is factory overhead "Actual" debited to record factory overhead?

- If all material goes into a materials account when purchased, then why is it designated direct or indirect material when it is taken out of the materials account?

- What is the difference between under- and overapplied factory overhead?

- Basically, job order is custom-ordered items from a customer. Then why is it necessary to keep up with all costs when an estimate has been given before the job is taken?

- Can a business use both process and job order costing?

- Why is it necessary to keep up with the flow of costs in a job order system?

- When we credit accumulated depreciation for the factory depreciation, why don't we debit depreciation expense?

# OBJECTIVE 1

**Describe cost accounting systems used by manufacturing businesses.**

## KEY TERMS

Cost Accounting Systems      Process Cost System
Job Order Cost System

## SUGGESTED APPROACH

Transparency Master (TM) 19-1 describes the focus and information provided by cost accounting systems. After reviewing this information, introduce students to job order and process cost systems. Emphasize that job order systems are used by companies that make custom, special-order type goods or produce a high variety of products. Process cost systems are used by companies that make "a whole bunch of stuff that all looks the same" under a continuous manufacturing process. Ask your students to name types of manufacturers that would make products suitable to a job order system (such as new-construction homes, replacement windows, class rings, business cards, and wedding invitations). Repeat this exercise to identify process cost manufacturers.

# OBJECTIVE 2

**Describe and illustrate a job order cost accounting system.**

## KEY TERMS

Activity Base      Materials Requisition
Activity-Based Costing      Overapplied Factory Overhead
Cost Allocation      Predetermined Factory Overhead Rate
Finished Goods Ledger      Receiving Report
Job Cost Sheets      Time Tickets
Materials Ledger      Underapplied Factory Overhead

## SUGGESTED APPROACH

Objective 2 introduces students to the various documents and procedures used in accumulating the accounting data under a job order system. Two different approaches to cover the documents in a job order system are described below.

## CLASS DISCUSSION — Information Needed in a Job Order System

Ask your students to assume that they manage the manufacturing operations for the custom order division of a company that makes fine jewelry. The company's raw materials consist mainly of gold (10 karat and 14 karat), precious stones, and semiprecious stones. Ask your students to describe manufacturing information that would be important to track. List their responses on the board.

Your students should list many of the following concerns. Point out the accounting documents used to gather and report this information.

| | |
|---|---|
| The amount of each type of material on hand | Materials Ledger — shows a record of the amount of each material on hand |
| The quantity of material used on each customer order | Materials Requisition — provides authorization for materials to be released from the inventory storage area; shows specific quantity of materials used in each customer order |
| The labor costs used on each customer order. | Time Tickets — filled out by employees; shows the amount of time spent working on each job and the labor cost |
| The total cost of making a customer's order | Job Cost Sheet — lists materials (from materials requisitions), labor costs (from time tickets), and overhead used on each customer job |
| The costs incurred on jobs currently in process | Cost Ledger — job cost sheets for all orders in process |
| The total cost of all completed jobs | Finished Goods Ledger — job cost sheets for all finished orders |

## CLASS DISCUSSION — Documents and Procedures in a Job Order System

You can also cover this objective through a bit of role playing. Tell your class to assume that they are workers for the custom order division of a manufacturer that makes fine jewelry. Assign specific manufacturing job responsibilities to various class members. Ask your students the questions listed below concerning the procedures and documents they would use in their jobs.

The goal is for students to understand the information needed by various manufacturing personnel and then attach a name to documents that report that information. You may need to be the person who attaches the name to the students' ideas. For example, when you ask the production scheduler how he or she will inform the storeroom clerk of the need for inventoried materials, he or she will probably suggest writing a note or memo. (If the production scheduler says, "I'd call the storeroom clerk," state that all requests need to be in writing because of the volume of requests for raw materials.) Next, ask the scheduler what information would be on the memo. Then you can attach a name to this memo; the document used to request that material is a materials requisition.

1. Appoint one of your students to be the production scheduler for your company. Whenever this student receives a customer order, he or she is to schedule when the item will be made. Tell that student to assume that the company has just received an order to make World Series rings for the winning baseball team. Ask him or her to name the steps that would need to be taken to schedule the job. The student should mention the following (with a little prodding from you, if necessary):
   a. Look at other jobs scheduled to see when workers will have time to start this job.
   b. Determine whether the materials are on hand to make the rings.

   Tell the student to assume that materials need to be ordered (the details of purchasing raw materials are not specifically described in this chapter, you may wish to skip to step 3 which is covered in the chapter). The company's purchasing agent orders all materials. Ask the student how he or she would tell the purchasing agent what to order. (Answer: Fill out a purchase requisition.)

2. Name one student as the purchasing agent. Ask what he or she would do after receiving the purchase requisition. (Answer: Fill out a purchase order and transmit it to the vendor.)

3. Appoint a student to be the receiving department. Ask what he or she would do when goods are received. (Answer: Inspect and count the items, fill out a receiving report, and take the materials to the storeroom.)

4. Name a storeroom supervisor. Ask this student what he or she would do when the materials are received. (Answer: Put them away, preferably where they are locked up.)

   Next, ask this student whether he or she would give materials to any employee who asked for them. What would the storeroom supervisor need in order to give materials to a production employee? (Answer: a materials requisition)

5. Ask one student to be the skilled craftsman who is going to make the rings. Tell the student that the company wants to know the labor cost of all orders. Ask what information he or she would record so the company could determine the labor cost. (Answer: The time spent working on the order would be recorded on a time ticket.)

6. Appoint one of your students as the accountant. That student needs to determine the cost to make the rings. Ask him or her to describe how to get the information to determine the cost. (Answer: Take materials used from the materials requisition and labor costs from the time tickets; these costs, along with overhead, are recorded on a job cost sheet.)

Ask the student how he or she could determine the costs spent on jobs that have been completed. (Answer: Add up the job cost sheets for all finished jobs. The job cost sheets for all finished jobs make up the finished goods ledger.)

Finally, ask the accountant how he or she could determine the costs spent on all jobs that are still being worked on. (Answer: Add up the job cost sheets for the jobs still in process. The job cost sheets for jobs in process make up the cost ledger.)

## LECTURE AID — Allocation of Overhead

In addition to direct materials cost and direct labor cost, objective 2 covers the allocation of overhead costs in a job order setting. The following example may be helpful in explaining why overhead costs need to be allocated.

Assume that you are responsible for planning a banquet for your school's accounting club. The banquet will feature a dinner, followed by a speaker. The costs associated with the banquet are as follows:

| | |
|---|---|
| Meals | $10 per person |
| Beverages (coffee and tea) | $1 per person |
| Use of banquet room | $50 |
| Speaker's fee | $100 |

Assume that 50 students will attend the banquet. If you want to break even on this event, how much do you need to charge for a ticket? (Answer: $14)

In this case, meals and beverages are costs that can be traced to each student attending the banquet. Fees paid for use of the room and to the speaker cannot be directly traced to each student. These costs must be allocated to each attendee in order to determine what it will cost each person to attend the banquet. The $150 in costs allocated over 50 people equals $3 per person.

## DEMONSTRATION PROBLEM — Allocation of Overhead

The costs of manufacturing a product that cannot be traced to a particular job are called overhead. Overhead costs must be allocated to the products made to determine what each product costs.

Point out that, unlike the situation in the banquet example, overhead costs usually are not divided evenly over the number of units produced. Assume that a television manufacturer spent $500,000 on overhead costs to make 50,000 televisions. At first glance, it might seem fair to allocate $10 in overhead to each television. But what if some televisions were big-screen stereo sets and some were small, portable models? It isn't fair to charge each set with the same overhead if some models are more complicated to manufacture than others.

Assume that MTM manufacturing estimates it will spend $1 million on overhead expenses. MTM is a highly automated manufacturing plant; therefore, the majority of its overhead expenses relate to machinery (depreciation, repairs and maintenance, electricity used). Machine hours used would be a reasonable way to allocate overhead costs to products because use of machinery causes (or drives) overhead expenses. MTM estimates that it will run its machines for 40,000 hours during the year.

The formula to calculate MTM's predetermined overhead rate is as follows:

$$\frac{\text{Estimated Total Factory Overhead Costs}}{\text{Estimated Activity Base (machine hours)}} = \frac{\$1,000,000}{40,000 \text{ hours}} = \$25/\text{hour}$$

In this case, $25 in overhead is allocated each time a product accumulates one hour of machine time.

Ask your students to calculate the overhead that would be allocated to a product that uses 3.5 hours of machine time. (Answer: $87.50) Remind students that overhead costs are added to the product's materials and labor costs.

Emphasize that the identification of the appropriate activity base or driver is essential to developing accurate product costs. If a highly automated manufacturer allocates overhead based on direct labor hours, the resulting product costs may be distorted. The activity base should be related to the incurrence of overhead costs.

In practice, more than one factory overhead rate may be used for applying overhead. Materials-related overhead (such as purchasing, materials receiving or inspection, and materials storage costs) could be allocated based on the direct materials cost of a product, with the remaining overhead allocated based on direct labor hours or machine hours. Using activity-based costing to allocate overhead is discussed and illustrated in Chapter 25.

## DEMONSTRATION PROBLEM — Overapplied and Underapplied Overhead

Ask your students to calculate the amount of overhead allocated to the products of a company that has a predetermined overhead rate of $10 per machine hour if machines were used for 10,000 hours. (Answer: $100,000)

What if the company actually spent $95,000 on overhead costs? The company has overapplied overhead of $5,000. A company may have overapplied or underapplied overhead if:

1. Actual overhead costs do not equal the estimated costs used to compute the predetermined overhead rate.
2. The actual activity base (machine hours) does not equal the estimated activity base used to compute the predetermined overhead rate.

TM 19-2 shows circumstances where over- and underapplied overhead occur and how they are treated in the accounting records.

## GROUP LEARNING ACTIVITY — Journal Entries in a Job Order System

Exhibit 2 in the text summarizes the flow of costs in a job order cost system (costs move from materials inventory to work in process to finished goods to cost of goods sold). Exhibit 8 shows the entries needed to record manufacturing costs in T accounts. Ask your students to record the journal entries listed on

TM 19-3, using Exhibits 2 and 8 as a guide. The correct entries are displayed on TM 19-4. You may want to have your students post these entries to T accounts and determine account balances.

Emphasize the following points as students record their entries:

1. Materials requisitions serve as the basis for transferring material costs from materials to work in process and factory overhead.
2. Actual overhead costs are debited to factory overhead. Applied overhead costs are credited to factory overhead.
3. Entries to work in process are supported by job cost sheets. At the end of the period, the sum of the totals from all job cost sheets that are still in process must equal the balance of work in process.
4. Product sales serve as the basis for transferring jobs from finished goods to cost of goods sold.

# OBJECTIVE 3

**Describe the use of job order cost information for decision making.**

## SUGGESTED APPROACH

The goal of this objective is to explore the ways in which job cost information is used in decision making. To put your students in the role of decision maker, use the following Group Learning Activity.

## GROUP LEARNING ACTIVITY — Decision Making

Handout 19-1 is a brief problem asking students to interpret two job cost sheets. Ask your students to work on this problem in groups. After providing sufficient time, ask some of the groups to report their responses. TM 19-5 provides the solution.

Comparing the two job cost sheets shows that the improved price per pound of alloy does not offset the increased costs associated with higher materials usage rates and reduced casting and machining department efficiency. It is likely that the events are related. The lower alloy cost has probably resulted from the purchase of sub-quality raw materials. As a result, more alloy is required per casting on Job 210 than on prior jobs. In addition, the casting and machining departments are having greater difficulty with the castings, causing the efficiency of the departments to drop. Therefore, it appears that the new alloy vendor is causing the company to experience more scrapped castings, which increases the materials cost and conversion costs to produce product. Shipping costs are unaffected.

Job 210 also is allocated more overhead because it now consumes more labor hours. This allocation appears logical, since the job probably requires more overhead resources. The cost of activities such as scheduling, production control, and quality have probably increased because of the greater unreliability of the casting operations, caused by the lower quality alloy.

# OBJECTIVE 4

Describe the flow of costs for a service business that uses a job order cost accounting system.

## SUGGESTED APPROACH

Explain that cost accounting can be applied to any organization that needs to determine the cost of its product. For a service business, the product is the service provided. Cost accounting can be used by an advertising agency to determine the cost to produce an ad for a customer, by an accountant to determine the cost of preparing a tax return, or by a plumber to determine the cost to clean a drain.

Refer your students to Exhibit 11 in the text. While reviewing that diagram, stress the following points:

1. The costs incurred by a service organization are labor and overhead. Any supplies used are treated as an overhead expense.
2. A cost of services account is used to record the cost of completed jobs.

## GROUP LEARNING ACTIVITY — Job Order Costing in a Service Business

TM 19-6 presents information about a CPA firm that does audit and tax work. Divide your class into small groups and instruct students to determine the cost to prepare a tax return. The solution is shown on TM 19-7.

**Handout 19-1**

# Decision Making Using Job Cost Data

Griffin Casting Company is a job shop that manufactures castings for a variety of purposes. The following two job cost sheets relate to two different orders for an identical casting used to house automobile generators. As can be seen from the two job cost sheets, the unit cost has increased between March and October. The purchasing manager has explained that the problem is not with the purchasing department. In October, purchasing was able to buy metal alloys from a new vendor at a price of $12 per pound, a savings of $3 per pound from the previous vendor used in March. The new vendor has not been quality certified.

Required: Interpret the job cost reports to determine what has caused the per unit cost increase.

**Job 100**     Date Completed: March 30       Item: 40 automobile generator housings

| Materials: | Quantity | Price | Amount |
|---|---|---|---|
| Alloy (pounds) | 60 | $15.00 | $900 |
| Fasteners | 160 | 0.25 | 40 |
| Total materials | | | $940 |

| Direct labor: | Hours | Rate | Amount |
|---|---|---|---|
| Casting | 20.00 | $14.00 | $280 |
| Machining | 40.00 | 16.00 | 640 |
| Shipping | 4.00 | 10.00 | 40 |
| Total direct labor | 64.00 | | $960 |
| Factory overhead | | | |
| (200% of direct labor dollars) | 960 × 200% | | $1,920 |
| Total Cost | | | $3,820 |
| Total Units | | | ÷ 40 |
| Unit Cost | | | $95.50 |

**Job 210**     Date Completed: October 15       Item: 100 automobile generator housings

| Materials: | Quantity | Price | Amount |
|---|---|---|---|
| Alloy (pounds) | 200 | $12.00 | $2,400 |
| Fasteners | 400 | 0.25 | 100 |
| Total materials | | | $2,500 |

| Direct labor: | Hours | Rate | Amount |
|---|---|---|---|
| Casting | 60.00 | $14.00 | $ 840 |
| Machining | 120.00 | 16.00 | 1,920 |
| Shipping | 10.00 | 10.00 | 100 |
| Total direct labor | 190.00 | | $2,860 |
| Factory overhead | | | |
| (200% of direct labor dollars) | 2,860 × 200% | | $5,720 |
| Total Cost | | | $11,080 |
| Total Units | | | ÷ 100 |
| Unit Cost | | | $110.80 |

# HOMEWORK CHART WITH LEARNING OUTCOMES TAGGING

| Problem | Learning Objective | Description | DIFFICULTY | BUSPROG Primary | ACBSP Primary | ACBSP Secondary | IMA Managerial Only | BLOOM'S | TIME | Spread-sheet | GL |
|---|---|---|---|---|---|---|---|---|---|---|---|
| DQ19-1 | 19-1 | | Easy | Analytic | Job Order Costing | | Cost Management | Knowledge | 5 min. | | |
| DQ19-2 | 19-1 | | Easy | Analytic | Job Order Costing | | Cost Management | Knowledge | 5 min. | | |
| DQ19-3 | 19-2 | | Easy | Analytic | Job Order Costing | | Cost Management | Knowledge | 5 min. | | |
| DQ19-4 | 19-2 | | Easy | Analytic | Job Order Costing | | Cost Management | Knowledge | 5 min. | | |
| DQ19-5 | 19-2 | | Easy | Analytic | Job Order Costing | | Cost Management | Knowledge | 5 min. | | |
| DQ19-6 | 19-2 | | Easy | Analytic | Job Order Costing | | Cost Management | Knowledge | 5 min. | | |
| DQ19-7 | 19-2 | | Easy | Analytic | Job Order Costing | | Cost Management | Knowledge | 5 min. | | |
| DQ19-8 | 19-2 | | Easy | Analytic | Job Order Costing | | Cost Management | Knowledge | 5 min. | | |
| DQ19-9 | 19-2 | | Easy | Analytic | Job Order Costing | | Cost Management | Knowledge | 5 min. | | |
| DQ19-10 | 19-4 | | Easy | Analytic | Job Order Costing | | Cost Management | Knowledge | 5 min. | | |
| PE19-1A | 19-2 | Issuance of materials | Easy | Analytic | Job Order Costing | | Cost Management | Application | 5 min. | | |
| PE19-1B | 19-2 | Issuance of materials | Easy | Analytic | Job Order Costing | | Cost Management | Application | 5 min. | | |
| PE19-2A | 19-2 | Direct labor costs | Easy | Analytic | Job Order Costing | | Cost Management | Application | 5 min. | | |
| PE19-2B | 19-2 | Direct labor costs | Easy | Analytic | Job Order Costing | | Cost Management | Application | 5 min. | | |
| PE19-3A | 19-2 | Factory overhead costs | Easy | Analytic | Job Order Costing | | Cost Management | Application | 5 min. | | |
| PE19-3B | 19-2 | Factory overhead costs | Easy | Analytic | Job Order Costing | | Cost Management | Application | 5 min. | | |
| PE19-4A | 19-2 | Applying factory overhead | Easy | Analytic | Job Order Costing | | Cost Management | Application | 10 min. | | |
| PE19-4B | 19-2 | Applying factory overhead | Easy | Analytic | Job Order Costing | | Cost Management | Application | 10 min. | | |
| PE19-5A | 19-2 | Job costs | Easy | Analytic | Job Order Costing | | Cost Management | Application | 10 min. | | |

| Problem | Learning Objective | Description | DIFFICULTY | EUSPROG Primary | ACBSP Primary | ACBSP Secondary | IMA Managerial Only | BLOOM'S | TIME | Spreadsheet | GL |
|---|---|---|---|---|---|---|---|---|---|---|---|
| PE19-5B | 19-2 | Job costs | Easy | Analytic | Job Order Costing | | Cost Management | Application | 10 min. | | |
| PE19-6A | 19-2 | Cost of goods sold | Easy | Analytic | Job Order Costing | | Cost Management | Application | 5 min. | | |
| PE19-6B | 19-2 | Cost of goods sold | Easy | Analytic | Job Order Costing | | Cost Management | Application | 5 min. | | |
| Ex19-1 | 19-2 | Transactions in a job order cost system | Easy | Analytic | Job Order Costing | | Cost Management | Knowledge | 5 min. | | |
| Ex19-2 | 19-2 | Cost flow relationships | Easy | Analytic | Job Order Costing | | Cost Management | Application | 10 min. | | |
| Ex19-3 | 19-2 | Cost of materials issuances under the FIFO method | Moderate | Analytic | Job Order Costing | | Cost Management | Application | 30 min. | X | |
| Ex19-4 | 19-2 | Entry for issuing materials | Easy | Analytic | Job Order Costing | | Cost Management | Application | 5 min. | | |
| Ex19-5 | 19-2 | Entries for materials | Moderate | Analytic | Job Order Costing | | Cost Management | Application | 30 min. | | |
| Ex19-6 | 19-2 | Entry for factory labor costs | Easy | Analytic | Job Order Costing | | Cost Management | Application | 5 min. | | |
| Ex19-7 | 19-2 | Entry for factory labor costs | Moderate | Analytic | Job Order Costing | | Cost Management | Application | 15 min. | | |
| Ex19-8 | 19-2 | Entries for direct labor and factory overhead | Easy | Analytic | Job Order Costing | | Cost Management | Application | 10 min. | | |
| Ex19-9 | 19-2 | Factory overhead rates, entries, and account balance | Moderate | Analytic | Job Order Costing | | Cost Management | Application | 30 min. | | |
| Ex19-10 | 19-2 | Predetermined factory overhead rate | Moderate | Analytic | Job Order Costing | | Cost Management | Application | 15 min. | | |
| Ex19-11 | 19-2 | Predetermined factory overhead rate | Moderate | Analytic | Job Order Costing | | Cost Management | Application | 15 min. | | |
| Ex19-12 | 19-2 | Entry for jobs completed; cost of unfinished jobs | Moderate | Analytic | Job Order Costing | | Cost Management | Application | 15 min. | | |
| Ex19-13 | 19-2 | Entries for factory costs and jobs completed | Moderate | Analytic | Job Order Costing | | Cost Management | Application | 30 min. | | |
| Ex19-14 | 19-2 | Financial statements of a manufacturing firm | Moderate | Analytic | Job Order Costing | Financial Statements | Cost Management | Application | 30 min. | X | |
| Ex19-15 | 19-3 | Decision making with job order costs | Moderate | Analytic | Job Order Costing | | Cost Management | Application | 1 hour | | |
| Ex19-16 | 19-3 | Decision making with job order costs | Moderate | Analytic | Job Order Costing | | Cost Management | Application | 30 min. | | |

| Problem | Learning Objective | Description | DIFFICULTY | BUSPROG Primary | ACBSP Primary | ACBSP Secondary | IMA Managerial Only | BLOOM'S | TIME | Spreadsheet | GL |
|---|---|---|---|---|---|---|---|---|---|---|---|
| Ex19-17 | 19-4 | Job order cost accounting entries for a service business | Moderate | Analytic | Job Order Costing | | Cost Management | Application | 1 hour | | |
| Ex19-18 | 19-4 | Job order cost accounting entries for a service business | Moderate | Analytic | Job Order Costing | | Cost Management | Application | 30 min. | | |
| Pr19-1A | 19-2 | Entries for costs in a job order cost system | Moderate | Analytic | Job Order Costing | | Cost Management | Application | 45 min. | X | X |
| Pr19-2A | 19-2 | Entries and schedules for unfinished jobs and completed jobs | Challenging | Analytic | Job Order Costing | | Cost Management | Application | 1.5 hours | X | X |
| Pr19-3A | 19-2, 19-3 | Job order cost sheet | Challenging | Analytic | Job Order Costing | | Cost Management | Application | 1 hour | X | |
| Pr19-4A | 19-2 | Analyzing manufacturing cost accounts | Challenging | Analytic | Job Order Costing | | Cost Management | Application | 1.5 hours | X | |
| Pr19-5A | 19-2 | Flow of costs and income statement | Challenging | Analytic | Job Order Costing | Financial Statements | Cost Management | Application | 1.5 hours | X | |
| Pr19-1B | 19-2 | Entries for costs in a job order cost system | Moderate | Analytic | Job Order Costing | | Cost Management | Application | 45 min. | X | X |
| Pr19-2B | 19-2 | Entries and schedules for unfinished jobs and completed jobs | Challenging | Analytic | Job Order Costing | | Cost Management | Application | 1.5 hours | X | X |
| Pr19-3B | 19-2, 19-3 | Job order cost sheet | Challenging | Analytic | Job Order Costing | | Cost Management | Application | 1 hour | X | |
| Pr19-4B | 19-2 | Analyzing manufacturing cost accounts | Challenging | Analytic | Job Order Costing | | Cost Management | Application | 1.5 hours | X | |
| Pr19-5B | 19-2 | Flow of costs and income statement | Challenging | Analytic | Job Order Costing | Financial Statements | Cost Management | Application | 1.5 hours | X | |
| CP19-1 | 19-2 | Managerial analysis | Easy | Analytic | Job Order Costing | | Cost Management | Analysis | 15 min. | | |
| CP19-2 | 19-3 | Job order decision making and rate deficiencies | Challenging | Analytic | Job Order Costing | | Cost Management | Analysis | 1 hour | | |
| CP19-3 | 19-2 | Factory overhead rate | Moderate | Analytic | Job Order Costing | | Cost Management | Analysis | 30 min. | | |
| CP19-4 | 19-2 | Recording manufacturing costs | Moderate | Analytic | Job Order Costing | | Cost Management | Application | 30 min. | | |
| CP19-5 | 19-2 | Predetermined overhead rates | Moderate | Analytic | Job Order Costing | | Cost Management | Application | 45 min. | | |

# Process Cost Systems

## OPENING COMMENTS

Chapter 20 completes the coverage of manufacturing accounting by introducing process costing. The text demonstrates process costing under the FIFO method. The average cost method is presented in the chapter's appendix. Chapter 20 also discusses the impact of just-in-time systems on manufacturing.

In this chapter, you need to consider which method(s) of process costing you will choose to cover in your class. When the FIFO method is presented in the chapter (Objectives 2 and 3), the manufacturing department adds materials at the beginning of production and conversion costs evenly throughout production. This requires two sets of equivalent unit calculations. When the average cost method is presented in the chapter appendix, the problems show materials and conversion costs both added evenly throughout production, requiring only one equivalent unit calculation. This assumption, along with the ability to commingle beginning work in process with units started and completed, greatly simplifies the computations related to process costing.

The average cost method will still allow you to communicate the concept of equivalent units. If you want to take a more conceptual approach, you could choose to only cover the average cost method and keep the calculations more streamlined. If you want to dig into process costing more fully, the FIFO method may be your choice. Carefully consider a decision to cover both methods. Coupling the two different methods with two different sets of underlying assumptions may be very confusing, causing students to resort to rote memorization rather than understanding the accounting procedures presented.

After studying the chapter, your students should be able to:

1. Describe process cost systems.

2. Prepare a cost of production report.

3. Journalize entries for transactions using a process cost system.

4. Describe and illustrate the use of cost of production reports for decision making.

5. Compare just-in-time processing with traditional manufacturing processing.

# STUDENT FAQS

- Why is it necessary to know the four steps of producing a cost of production report?

- What does equivalent units of production (EUP) mean, and why is it necessary for it to be correct?

- Started and completed under "units to be assigned cost" gives me problems every time. Do you have a suggestion to eliminate my problem?

- Why does the complement of the percentage in beginning inventory have to be used to calculate EUP when the percent of completed has to be used for the ending?

- Why is just-in-time (JIT) processing meant to cut out all waste of cost in manufacturing?

- Why do we do a material and conversion EUP only? Shouldn't conversion be made into Direct Labor and Factory Overhead to be more accurate?

- 

# OBJECTIVE 1

Describe process cost systems.

## KEY TERMS

Process Cost System          Process Manufacturer

## SUGGESTED APPROACH

Transparency Masters (TMs) 20-1 through 20-3 explain the types of manufacturers that use job order and process costing, as well as the similarities and differences in these two systems. Ask your students to give examples of companies that would use job order costing and companies that would use process costing. As an alternative, ask your students whether a soft drink bottler would use a process or job order system.

Because costs are accumulated by department in a process cost system, each department has its own work in process account. Use TM 20-4 to explain the flow of costs through the departmental work in process accounts. Exhibit 3 in the text presents another illustration to reinforce the cost flows for a process manufacturer.

As you cover these illustrations, emphasize that there are separate work in process and factory overhead accounts for each department. This allows the manufacturer to accumulate product costs by department. Also stress that costs transferred out of one department become the costs transferred in to the next department.

# OBJECTIVE 2

Prepare a cost of production report.

## KEY TERMS

Cost of Production Report
Cost per Equivalent Unit
Equivalent Units of Production

First-in, First-out (FIFO) Method
Whole Units

## SUGGESTED APPROACH

TM 20-3 illustrates that each department in a process costing system can compute the cost to manufacture one unit of product as follows:

$$\text{Cost to Make One Unit in One Department} = \frac{\text{Department's Cost for the Month}}{\text{Number of Units Produced During the Month}}$$

The denominator of this equation assumes that whole units are completed during the month. However, this usually is not the case. As a result, companies are forced to calculate equivalent units. Equivalent units are the number of whole units that could have been made using the same manufacturing effort. Explain the calculation of equivalent units and show how it is used in determining product costs.

## GROUP LEARNING ACTIVITY — Cost of Production Report

Divide the class into small groups. Ask them to use the information and calculations from the demonstration problem in TM 20-5 to prepare a cost of production report for Advanced Technologics' assembly department. Refer your students to Exhibit 7 in the text as a model for this report. You may want to review the major sections of the cost of production report prior to assigning this activity.

A completed cost of production report is shown on TMs 20-12 and 20-13.

## LECTURE AID — Equivalent Units

The following scenario relates equivalent units to a common student dilemma.

Assume that you are taking four classes this term, and all four classes require a five-page paper. Of course, when will these papers be due? (I've never had a class that didn't immediately respond with the following answer: the same day.) OK, if these papers are all due the same day, when will you start them? (Once again, they always say: the night before they're due.)

Assume that you write four pages on the first paper and run out of information. Then you write three pages on the next paper and stop to watch a TV show. Next, you write two pages on the third paper before you get too bored to continue. So you switch to the last paper and write one page before you fall asleep at the keyboard. If you worked on one paper until it was finished and then started another paper, how many papers would you have completed? (Answer: two papers—finished a total of ten pages)

Emphasize that there are two equivalent units in this example. Two finished papers could have been written with the same effort used to do partial work on four papers.

# DEMONSTRATION PROBLEM — Process Costing, FIFO Method

The text presents the calculation of product costs under FIFO process costing as a four-step process. Use the following facts to demonstrate process costing (also on TM 20-5). This information refers to Advanced Technologies, the three-department computer manufacturer described on TM 20-4.

Advanced Technologies produces notebook computers in three departments: assembly, testing, and packing. Prior to the start of the production process, all the materials and component parts needed to assemble a computer are placed into a "kit." Manufacturing begins when the assembly department receives a kit and begins putting the computer together. Therefore, all materials are added at the beginning of work in the assembly department. Conversion costs are added evenly throughout the assembly process.

Assume that the assembly department of Advanced Technologies began April with 800 units in its work in process inventory. Assembly on these units was three-fourths complete at the beginning of the month. During the month, 3,000 units were started in the assembly department. At the end of the month, 300 of the units started were still in process; assembly on these units was two-thirds complete.

The costs associated with production in assembly during April were as follows:

| | |
|---|---|
| Cost of units in beginning work in process inventory | $228,000 |
| Cost of materials used in April | 630,000 |
| Cost of direct labor and overhead for April | 527,000 |

**STEP 1:** Determine the units to be assigned costs. Instruct students to begin by determining the total number of units worked on in the assembly department during April plus the number of units in each of the following three categories:

Beginning Work in Process Inventory

Units Started and Completed During the Month

Ending Work in Process Inventory

For example, Advanced Technologies worked on 3,800 units during April (the 800 in beginning work in process plus the 3,000 units started this month.) There were 800 units in beginning work in process inventory, 2,700 started and completed (3,000 started – 300 not completed) and 300 in ending work in process inventory.

**STEP 2:** Calculate equivalent units of production. Since all materials are added by the assembly department at the beginning of production, and conversion costs are added evenly throughout production, equivalent units must be calculated separately for materials and conversion costs. Remind students that conversion costs are the costs needed to "convert" raw materials to a finished product (labor and factory overhead). The calculation of equivalent units can be summarized in the following equation:

No. of Whole Units × Amount of Work Put into the Units during the Month
(expressed as a fraction or a percentage)

Material equivalent units for Advanced Technologies' assembly department would be calculated as follows:

|  | Whole Units | % Materials Added in April | Equivalent Units |
|---|---|---|---|
| Beginning WIP Inventory | 800 | 0 | 0 |
| Units Started and Completed | 2,700 | 100% | 2,700 |
| Ending WIP Inventory | 300 | 100% | 300 |
|  |  |  | 3,000 |

Emphasize that all materials are added at the beginning of production. Therefore, no materials are added to the beginning work in process inventory, which was placed into production last month.

Conversion equivalent units for Advanced Technologies' assembly department would be calculated as follows:

|  | Whole Units | % Conversion Added in April | Equivalent Units |
|---|---|---|---|
| Beginning WIP Inventory | 800 | 1/4 | 200 |
| Units Started and Completed | 2,700 | 100% | 2,700 |
| Ending WIP Inventory | 300 | 2/3 | 200 |
|  |  |  | 3,100 |

Emphasize that the percentage of completion can also be expressed as a fraction.

**STEP 3:** Determine the cost per equivalent unit. In order to determine the total cost to produce a unit, a manufacturer must compute the materials cost and the conversion cost (labor and overhead) in a completed unit. This amount is the cost per equivalent unit. The formula for this calculation is:

$$\text{Cost per Equivalent Unit} = \frac{\text{Costs Incurred During the Month}}{\text{Equivalent Units Produced During the Month}}$$

For Advanced Technologies, cost per equivalent unit must be calculated separately for materials and conversion costs since these resources are added at different rates in the manufacturing process (materials are added all at the beginning and conversion costs evenly throughout the process).

Materials and conversion costs per equivalent unit are calculated as follows:

$$\text{Materials Cost/Equivalent Unit} = \frac{\$630,000}{3,000 \text{ equiv. units}} = \$210$$

$$\text{Conversion Cost/Equivalent Unit} = \frac{\$527,000}{3,100 \text{ equiv. units}} = \$170$$

**STEP 4:** Allocate costs to transferred and partially completed units. After calculating the cost per equivalent unit for materials and conversion costs, the cost of units completed and those still in process must be determined. Stress that students will have the most success if they calculate the cost separately for each category of units on the equivalent units' schedule. The beginning work in process and started and completed categories represent units that have been completed in assembly and transferred on to the testing department. The ending work in process represents the units that have not been completed.

The cost assigned to the units that were in beginning work in process is:

|                          | Direct Materials | Conversion Cost | Total Cost |
|--------------------------|------------------|-----------------|------------|
| Beginning WIP Balance    |                  |                 | $228,000   |
| Cost to Complete:        |                  |                 |            |
| Equivalent Units for April | 0              | 200             |            |
| Cost per Equivalent Unit | × $210           | × $170          |            |
|                          | 0                | 34,000          | 34,000     |
| Cost of April 1 WIP      |                  |                 |            |
| transferred to testing   |                  |                 | $262,000   |

The cost assigned to the units that were started and completed in April is:

|                          | Direct Materials | Conversion Cost | Total Cost |
|--------------------------|------------------|-----------------|------------|
| Started and Completed:   |                  |                 |            |
| Equivalent Units         | 2,700            | 2,700           |            |
| Cost per Equivalent Unit | × $210           | × $170          |            |
| Cost of Units Started &  | $567,000         | $459,000        | $1,026,000 |
| Completed in April       |                  |                 |            |

Remind students that the total cost of units completed and transferred to testing is $1,288,000 ($262,000 + $1,026,000). This amount must be transferred from the work in process account for the assembly department to the testing department's work in process account. Note that the journal entry is covered in Objective 3.

| | | |
|---|---|---|
| WIP Inventory—Testing Department | 1,288,000 | |
|     WIP Inventory—Assembly Department | | 1,288,000 |

The cost assigned to the units that were in ending work in process inventory on April 30 is:

|  | Direct Materials | Conversion Cost | Total Cost |
|---|---|---|---|
| Ending WIP Inventory: |  |  |  |
| Equivalent Units | 300 | 200 |  |
| Cost per Equivalent Unit | × $210 | × $170 |  |
| Total Cost of Ending WIP | $63,000 | $34,000 | $97,000 |

## CLASS DISCUSSION — Process Costing

In the previous Demonstration Problem, all materials were introduced at the beginning of the production process. Ask your students for other examples of materials that would be added at the start of production. Additional ideas include soup broth for soup making, alumina for aluminum smelting, crude oil for gasoline refining, or pulp for papermaking. Next ask your students for materials that would not be added at the beginning of the manufacturing process. Examples include icing for cake baking, varnish for making wood furniture, or packing material for any product delivered in a box.

In the Advanced Technologies problem, all conversion costs were incurred evenly throughout the production process. Ask your students for an example of an overhead cost that would not be incurred evenly. One example would be energy costs. Frequently, the energy component is not used at exactly the same rate throughout processing. Therefore, some companies separate the energy cost from conversion costs and account for it separately.

## GROUP LEARNING ACTIVITY — Process Costing with Transferred in Costs, FIFO Method

The textbook illustrates process costing for the first department in a manufacturing process. End of chapter problems also ask students to calculate product costs for departments that are second or third in the manufacturing flow. Emphasize that all departments that receive units from prior departments also receive costs that are "transferred in" from those departments. Transferred in costs can be treated in the same manner as materials added at the beginning of the production process.

TM 20-6 presents information to calculate and assign costs to units in Advanced Technology's testing department for the month of April. The four-step solution to this problem is provided on TMs 20-7 through 20-11. Allow your students the opportunity to practice FIFO process costing by working in groups. Since most students struggle with this topic, the time for group work is well spent.

# OBJECTIVE 3

Journalize entries for transactions using a process cost system.

## SUGGESTED APPROACH

A process cost system requires only a few modifications to the journal entries illustrated for a job order manufacturer in Chapter 19. These modifications are as follows:

1. Separate work in process accounts are maintained for each department.

2. Separate factory overhead accounts are maintained for each department.

3. To determine the cost of units transferred from one production department to the next department (or to finished goods), equivalent units must be computed and costs assigned using the method illustrated under Objective 2.

Refer students to the journal entries illustrated in the text. Stress that a cost of production report or four-step process costing calculation must be prepared to determine the cost of units transferred to the various departments and the cost of completed units transferred to finished goods.

It would be an excellent learning activity to ask your students to work in groups to complete a process costing problem and all related journal entries at this point. However, that activity would be extremely lengthy. As an alternative, give your students the opportunity to start a homework assignment requiring journal entries (such as Problem 20-1A or 20-1B) in class. This will allow them to ask any questions necessary to get started on the "right foot."

# OBJECTIVE 4

Describe and illustrate the use of cost of production reports for decision making.

## KEY TERM

Yield

## SUGGESTED APPROACH

The objective in this section is to move the students from preparing cost reports to using them for decision making. A manufacturing cost system provides the user with a database of cost information. This database can be used to segment cost data in a number of ways, such as by product, by process, by production line, or by work shift. This detail gives manufacturers the ability to discover the root causes of cost problems. Use the Group Learning Activity below to develop these issues in class.

You may also want to point out that the cost of production report illustrated in the text is highly summarized. In a real-world setting, each significant material and energy input would be individually identified. In most cases, conversion costs are not lumped together but would be individually identified as well.

## GROUP LEARNING ACTIVITY — Decision Making Exercise

Provide students with Handout 20-1. This handout describes a situation where material costs have been stratified by line and by shift. This information will give students an opportunity to think in relational database terms. There are often a number of different ways to view data. Asking for the right view and then interpreting the patterns that you see is part of the role of a business analyst. The solution to Handout 20-1 is provided in TM 20-14.

# OBJECTIVE 5
### Compare just-in-time processing with traditional manufacturing processing.

## KEY TERMS

Just-in-Time (JIT) Processing            Manufacturing Cells

## SUGGESTED APPROACH

Just-in-time (JIT) manufacturing is not just a method of reducing inventory. It is embraced as a philosophy that emphasizes eliminating waste from all processes. Inventory is simply a buffer that protects a process against unreliability (such as poor supplier delivery or machinery that breaks down frequently). Reducing inventory levels without correcting the problems that create unreliability will stop production. Constructing a reliable system will eliminate the need for an inventory buffer.

Exhibits 9 and 10 in the text illustrate the production line and flow of products under a traditional and a JIT system. Review these diagrams with your students and emphasize the following points.

1. JIT organizes work cells that perform several manufacturing steps. Workers are cross-trained to perform more than one task. This allows manufacturing to be more flexible and gives workers more pride in the final product.

2. Because products do not move between as many departments, the non-value-added cost of transporting products and parts is reduced.

Emphasize that the employee involvement in a JIT system also implies employee accountability. Employees cannot be either involved or accountable without information. If employees are to be accountable for financial performance, then they will need access to financial information. Therefore, financial information cannot be limited to managers in a JIT organization. All employees must have access and be trained to interpret financial data.

## IN-CLASS SIMULATION — Just-in-Time Manufacturing

Just-in-time is essentially a demand-pull system. Products are not made until they are needed by the customer, and component parts are not made until they are needed by the next stage of production. Just-in-time significantly reduces inventories, allowing manufacturers to reduce costs incurred in moving and storing inventory. Just-in-time also emphasizes quality.

You can simulate the difference between the traditional push system and the demand-pull system of just-in-time in your classroom. You will need scrap paper, four pens, a stapler, and six volunteers. Divide the scrap paper between two volunteers. Instruct one student to write an "A" on his or her pieces of paper, and ask the other to write a "B." Use another volunteer as an expediter to collect the completed A and B papers and carry them to a fourth volunteer, who staples the papers together. The fifth volunteer picks up the stapled sets of paper and delivers them to the sixth volunteer—the customer.

As a first simulation, instruct all volunteers to do their assigned tasks as quickly as possible. Tell them to focus on quantity and ignore quality. Allow them to work for 30 seconds, then stop the production line. Announce that the customer wants to change the color of the ink used to write the As and Bs, effective immediately. Therefore, any work in process will need to be scrapped. Count the scrapped sheets. Allow your students to work for another 30 seconds. Ask your customer to count the completed products he or she received.

Run this simulation a second time, but this time institute a demand-pull system. Instruct all workers that they are not to make a new product (or component) until it is needed for the next stage of production. Also ask them to focus on quality, not quantity. In addition, physically move the students who are writing letters close enough to the student stapling the papers so that an expediter is not needed to move the papers from one station to the next. Allow your students to work for 30 seconds. After that time, stop production, announce another ink color change, and collect any work in process as scrap. Start up the production line again for another 30 seconds. Ask your customer to count the completed products received.

You should find that the number of completed units is about the same under either system. However, the amount of scrap will be dramatically reduced under the just-in-time system. In addition, you may want to ask your customer to compare the quality of the output. It should be significantly higher under the second simulation.

## LECTURE AID — Value-Added versus Non-Value-Added

Each activity performed by an organization creates cost. If the activity does not create any value for the customer, its cost represents wasted resources and it can be labeled as "non-value-added." Since one of the goals of a JIT system is to eliminate waste, non-value-added activities should be identified and eliminated, if possible.

The following questions can aid students in determining if an activity is value-added or non-value-added.

1. Given a choice, would the customer pay for this activity?

2. If you quit performing this activity, would the customer care?

3. If you quit performing this activity, would the output still meet customer requirements?

4. Could you eliminate this activity if some other activity were done correctly or differently?

5. Would reengineering the system eliminate this activity?

A "yes" answer to questions 1 or 2 indicates a value-added activity. A "yes" answer to questions 3, 4, or 5 indicates a non-value-added activity.

# APPENDIX — AVERAGE COST METHOD

## SUGGESTED APPROACH

If you are going to present only the average cost method of process costing, you will want to start by thoroughly explaining the need for equivalent units. Begin by using TM 20-3 to illustrate that each department in a process costing system can compute the cost to manufacture one unit of product as follows:

$$\text{Cost to Make One Unit in One Department} = \frac{\text{Department's Cost for the Month}}{\text{Number of Units Produced During the Month}}$$

The denominator of this equation assumes that whole units are completed during the month. However, this usually is not the case. As a result, companies are forced to calculate equivalent units. Equivalent units are the number of whole units that could have been made using the same manufacturing effort. Refer to the section entitled "LECTURE AIDS — Equivalent Units" under Objective 3 for material to help you explain the concept of equivalent units. Then, use the following demonstration problem to present the four steps to solve an average cost process costing problem.

## DEMONSTRATION PROBLEM — Process Costing, Average Cost Method

Use the following facts to demonstrate process costing (also on TM 20-15).

Healthy Harvest Company is a bakery that makes breads. The manufacturing department is organized into three departments: dough making, baking, and packaging. The following information is related to the dough making department:

Cost data for the month of April:

| | |
|---|---|
| Work in process inventory, April 1 (100 units, 40 percent complete) | $ 49.00 |
| Direct materials cost (for 2,050 units) | 400.00 |
| Direct labor cost | 80.00 |
| Factory overhead applied | 220.00 |
| Total production costs | $749.00 |

Unit data:

| | |
|---|---|
| Units transferred to baking in April | 2,100 |
| Units in work in process on April 30 (80 percent complete) | 50 |

**STEP 1:** Determine the units to be assigned costs. In this step, students determine the total number of units worked on in the dough-making department during April from both an "Input" and an "Output" perspective.

The Input Perspective:

| | |
|---|---|
| Units in work in process, April 1 | 100 |
| Units started in production, based on materials requisitioned | 2,050 |
| Total units to be accounting for | 2,150 |

The Output Perspective:

| | |
|---|---|
| Units transferred out to the next department (baking) | 2,100 |
| Units in work in process, April 30 | 50 |
| Total units to be accounting for | 2,150 |

In reality, the preceding calculations only use the numbers identified under the "Output" perspective.

**STEP 2:** Calculate equivalent units of production. In the textbook problems and exercises based on the chapter appendix, students must assume that materials and conversion costs are added evenly throughout production. Therefore, only one equivalent unit calculation is required. If you have not covered the FIFO method, students won't be expecting two equivalent unit calculations (one for materials and one for conversion costs), so you won't even need to mention this assumption.

In the average cost method, the calculation of equivalent units can be summarized in the following equation:

No. of Whole Units × Percent of these units complete at the end of the month
(expressed as a fraction or a percentage)

Equivalent units for Healthy Harvests' dough-making department would be calculated as follows:

| | |
|---|---|
| Equivalent units transferred to baking in April (2,100 × 100%) | 2,100 |
| Equivalent units in work in process on April 30 (50 × 80%) | 40 |
| Total equivalent units | 2,140 |

Emphasize that the equivalent units for the ending work in process is 40 because doing 80 percent of the work on 50 units takes the same resources as doing 100 percent of the work on 40 units.

**STEP 3:** Determine the cost per equivalent unit. The formula for this calculation is:

$$\text{Cost per Equivalent Unit} = \frac{\text{Total Production Costs}}{\text{Total Equivalent Units}}$$

Continuing with the data for Healthy Harvest, the cost per equivalent unit is:

$$\text{Cost/Equivalent Unit} = \frac{\$749}{2{,}140 \text{ equiv. units}} = \$0.35$$

**STEP 4:** Allocate costs to transferred and partially completed units. In this step, students calculate the cost that is transferred to the baking department and the costs that remain in the dough-making department's work in process account. For each of those categories, the costs are determined as follows:

$$\text{\# of equivalent units} \times \text{cost per equivalent unit}$$

Using the data from Healthy Harvest:

| | |
|---|---|
| Costs transferred to the baking department | |
| (2,100 equivalent units × $0.35) | $735 |
| Costs of dough making's WIP on April 30 | |
| (40 equivalent units × $0.35) | 14 |
| Total production costs assigned | $749 |

From a journal entry perspective, $735 is transferred from WIP-dough making to WIP-baking. The balance remaining in WIP-dough making after this entry is posted would be $14.

## GROUP LEARNING ACTIVITY — Process Costing Using the Average Cost Method

TM 20-16 presents data for Healthy Harvest's baking department for the month of April. Ask your students to perform the four-step process costing calculations using the average cost method. The solution is on TMs 20-17 and 20-18.

Next, ask students to prepare a cost of production report using text Exhibit 11 as a model. The cost of production report simply shows the calculations on TMs 20-17 and 20-18 in a different format. Use the numbers on these TMs to check your students' work.

# Decision Making Using Process Cost Data

Hall Company produces synthetic materials from a chemical extrusion processes. Management has been concerned that material costs per pound are too high. Hall produces only a single product on four separate extrusion lines. The product is processed over two shifts per day. The following data have been collected for analysis:

January

| | |
|---|---|
| Total materials costs................................................................... | $335,050 |
| Total number of pounds produced................................................... | 50,400 |
| Cost per pound ......................................................................... | $6.65 |

Materials Costs by Production Line

| | Line 1 | Line 2 | Line 3 | Line 4 | Total |
|---|---|---|---|---|---|
| Shift 1.................................. | $36,000 | $36,000 | $40,300 | $36,000 | $148,300 |
| Shift 2.................................. | 45,500 | 45,500 | 50,250 | 45,500 | 186,750 |
| Total.................................... | $81,500 | $81,500 | $90,550 | $81,500 | $335,050 |

Pounds Produced by Production Line

| | Line 1 | Line 2 | Line 3 | Line 4 | Total |
|---|---|---|---|---|---|
| Shift 1.................................. | 6,000 | 6,000 | 6,200 | 6,000 | 24,200 |
| Shift 2.................................. | 6,500 | 6,500 | 6,700 | 6,500 | 26,200 |
| Total.................................... | 12,500 | 12,500 | 12,900 | 12,500 | 50,400 |

Assume you have interviewed the following individuals in an attempt to discover the problems causing material costs to be inflated: Juanita Marcos, shift 1 supervisor; Ed Curcek, shift 2 supervisor; and Hal Bundy, plant manager. A summary of their responses are given below.

**Hal:** I just received a directive from headquarters to increase my production rates. I talked to Ed and Juanita about kicking up our production from our old average of 6,000 pounds per shift. Juanita did not seem to think that this was a good idea. My bet is that our problems are with Juanita's shift.

**Juanita:** I have decided to keep first-shift production on lines 1, 2, and 4 at 6,000 pounds per shift. That's because I remember the last time we had our production rates increased. Our materials consumption shot through the roof. Therefore, I'm running a small experiment on Line 3 before increasing the speeds across the whole shift. I know Ed has increased production on the second shift, but he was just brought in from another plant that has new machinery. I don't expect he's had the historical experience with these older machines that I've had.

**Ed:** I've increased production rates on my shift, but it's hard to tell how things are going. I thought the new directive made plenty of sense. Back at my previous plant location, we ran machines at 7,000 pounds per shift without any trouble. These older machines don't seem to be running nearly as well as the machines back at my old place. I guess when we see the numbers at the end of the month we'll have a good feel for it.

**Required:** Provide an analysis of the data that will assist the management of Hall Company determine whether or not the increase in production rates is having a favorable impact on production costs.

# HOMEWORK CHART WITH LEARNING OUTCOMES TAGGING

| Problem | Learning Objective | Description | DIFFICULTY | BUS-PROG Primary | ACBSP Primary | ACBSP Secondary | IMA Managerial Only | BLOOM'S | TIME | Spread-sheet | GL |
|---|---|---|---|---|---|---|---|---|---|---|---|
| DQ20-1 | 20-1 | | Easy | Analytic | Process Costing | Job Order Costing | Cost Management | Knowledge | 5 min. | | |
| DQ20-2 | 20-1 | | Easy | Analytic | Process Costing | Job Order Costing | Cost Management | Knowledge | 5 min. | | |
| DQ20-3 | 20-1 | | Easy | Analytic | Process Costing | | Cost Management | Knowledge | 5 min. | | |
| DQ20-4 | 20-2 | | Easy | Analytic | Process Costing | | Cost Management | Knowledge | 5 min. | | |
| DQ20-5 | 20-2 | | Easy | Analytic | Process Costing | | Cost Management | Knowledge | 5 min. | | |
| DQ20-6 | 20-3 | | Easy | Analytic | Process Costing | | Cost Management | Knowledge | 5 min. | | |
| DQ20-7 | 20-4 | | Easy | Analytic | Process Costing | | Cost Management | Knowledge | 5 min. | | |
| DQ20-8 | 20-4 | | Easy | Analytic | Process Costing | | Cost Management | Knowledge | 5 min. | | |
| DQ20-9 | 20-4 | | Easy | Analytic | Process Costing | | Cost Management | Knowledge | 5 min. | | |
| DQ20-10 | 20-5 | | Easy | Analytic | Process Costing | | Cost Management | Knowledge | 5 min. | | |
| PE20-1A | 20-1 | Job order vs. process costing | Easy | Analytic | Process Costing | Job Order Costing | Cost Management | Knowledge | 5 min. | | |
| PE20-1B | 20-1 | Job order vs. process costing | Easy | Analytic | Process Costing | Job Order Costing | Cost Management | Knowledge | 5 min. | | |
| PE20-2A | 20-2 | Units to be assigned costs | Easy | Analytic | Process Costing | | Cost Management | Application | 5 min. | | |
| PE20-2B | 20-2 | Units to be assigned costs | Easy | Analytic | Process Costing | | Cost Management | Application | 5 min. | | |
| PE20-3A | 20-2 | Equivalent units of materials cost | Easy | Analytic | Process Costing | | Cost Management | Application | 5 min. | | |
| PE20-3B | 20-2 | Equivalent units of materials cost | Easy | Analytic | Process Costing | | Cost Management | Application | 5 min. | | |
| PE20-4A | 20-2 | Equivalent units of conversion costs | Easy | Analytic | Process Costing | | Cost Management | Application | 5 min. | | |

| Problem | Learning Objective | Description | DIFFICULTY | BUSPROG Primary | ACBSP Primary | ACBSP Secondary | IMA Managerial Only | BLOOM'S | TIME | Spread-sheet | GL |
|---|---|---|---|---|---|---|---|---|---|---|---|
| PE20-4B | 20-2 | Equivalent units of conversion costs | Easy | Analytic | Process Costing | | Cost Management | Application | 5 min. | | |
| PE20-5A | 20-2 | Cost per equivalent unit | Easy | Analytic | Process Costing | | Cost Management | Application | 5 min. | | |
| PE20-5B | 20-2 | Cost per equivalent unit | Easy | Analytic | Process Costing | | Cost Management | Application | 5 min. | | |
| PE20-6A | 20-2 | Cost of units transferred out and ending work in process | Easy | Analytic | Process Costing | | Cost Management | Application | 10 min. | | |
| PE20-6B | 20-2 | Cost of units transferred out and ending work in process | Easy | Analytic | Process Costing | | Cost Management | Application | 10 min. | | |
| PE20-7A | 20-3 | Process cost journal entries | Easy | Analytic | Process Costing | | Cost Management | Application | 10 min. | | |
| PE20-7B | 20-3 | Process cost journal entries | Easy | Analytic | Process Costing | | Cost Management | Application | 10 min. | | |
| PE20-8A | 20-4 | Using process costs for decision making | Easy | Analytic | Process Costing | | Cost Management | Application | 5 min. | | |
| PE20-8B | 20-4 | Using process costs for decision making | Easy | Analytic | Process Costing | | Cost Management | Application | 5 min. | | |
| Ex20-1 | 20-1, 20-3 | Entries for materials cost flows in a process cost system | Easy | Analytic | Process Costing | | Cost Management | Knowledge | 5 min. | | |
| Ex20-2 | 20-1 | Flowchart of accounts related to service and processing departments | Easy | Analytic | Process Costing | | Cost Management | Knowledge | 5 min. | | |
| Ex20-3 | 20-1, 20-3 | Entries for flow of factory costs for process cost system | Easy | Analytic | Process Costing | | Cost Management | Application | 10 min. | | |
| Ex20-4 | 20-1, 20-3 | Factory overhead rate, entry for applying factory overhead, and factory overhead account balance | Easy | Analytic | Process Costing | | Cost Management | Application | 10 min. | | |
| Ex20-5 | 20-2 | Equivalent units of production | Easy | Analytic | Process Costing | | Cost Management | Application | 5 min. | | |
| Ex20-6 | 20-2 | Equivalent units of production | Moderate | Analytic | Process Costing | | Cost Management | Application | 15 min. | | |
| Ex20-7 | 20-2 | Equivalent units of production | Moderate | Analytic | Process Costing | | Cost Management | Application | 15 min. | | |
| Ex20-8 | 20-2, 20-4 | Cost per equivalent unit | Moderate | Analytic | Process Costing | | Cost Management | Application | 30 min. | | |
| Ex20-9 | 20-2 | Equivalent units of production | Moderate | Analytic | Process Costing | | Cost Management | Application | 10 min. | | |

| Problem | Learning Objective | Description | DIFFICULTY | BUSPROG Primary | ACBSP Primary | ACBSP Secondary | IMA Managerial Only | BLOOM'S | TIME | Spread-sheet |
|---|---|---|---|---|---|---|---|---|---|---|
| Ex20-10 | 20-2 | Costs per equivalent unit | Moderate | Analytic | Process Costing | | Cost Management | Application | 15 min. | |
| Ex20-11 | 20-2 | Equivalent units of production and related costs | Moderate | Analytic | Process Costing | | Cost Management | Application | 15 min | X |
| Ex20-12 | 20-2, 20-4 | Cost of units completed and in process | Moderate | Analytic | Process Costing | | Cost Management | Application | 30 min. | |
| Ex20-13 | 20-2 | Errors in equivalent unit computation | Moderate | Analytic | Process Costing | | Cost Management | Application | 20 min. | |
| Ex20-14 | 20-2 | Cost per equivalent unit | Moderate | Analytic | Process Costing | | Cost Management | Application | 15 min. | |
| Ex20-15 | 20-2, 20-4 | Costs per equivalent unit and production costs | Moderate | Analytic | Process Costing | | Cost Management | Application | 30 min. | |
| Ex20-16 | 20-2, 20-4 | Cost of production report | Moderate | Analytic | Process Costing | | Cost Management | Application | 20 min. | X |
| Ex20-17 | 20-2, 20-4 | Cost of production report | Moderate | Analytic | Process Costing | | Cost Management | Application | 20 min. | |
| Ex20-18 | 20-1, 20-2, 20-3, 20-4 | Cost of production and journal entries | Moderate | Analytic | Process Costing | | Cost Management | Application | 30 min. | |
| Ex20-19 | 20-1, 20-2, 20-3 | Cost of production and journal entries | Moderate | Analytic | Process Costing | | Cost Management | Application | 20 min. | |
| Ex20-20 | 20-4 | Decision making | Moderate | Analytic | Process Costing | | Cost Management | Analysis | 20 min. | X |
| Ex20-21 | 20-4 | Decision making | Moderate | Analytic | Process Costing | | Cost Management | Evaluation | 20 min. | |
| Ex20-22 | 20-5 | Just-in-time manufacturing | Moderate | Analytic | Process Costing | | Strategic Planning | Analysis | 20 min. | |
| Ex20-23 | Appendix | Equivalent units of production: average cost method | Easy | Analytic | Process Costing | | Cost Management | Application | 20 min. | |
| Ex20-24 | Appendix | Equivalent units of production: average cost method | Moderate | Analytic | Process Costing | | Cost Management | Application | 20 min. | |
| Ex20-25 | Appendix | Equivalent units of production: average cost method | Moderate | Analytic | Process Costing | | Cost Management | Application | 20 min. | |
| Ex20-26 | Appendix | Equivalent units of production and related costs | Moderate | Analytic | Process Costing | | Cost Management | Application | 30 min. | X |
| Ex20-27 | Appendix | Cost per equivalent unit: average cost method | Moderate | Analytic | Process Costing | | Cost Management | Application | 20 min. | |

| Problem | Learning Objective | Description | DIFFICULTY | BUSPROG Primary | ACBSP Primary | ACBSP Secondary | IMA Managerial Only | BLOOM'S | TIME | Spread-sheet | GL |
|---|---|---|---|---|---|---|---|---|---|---|---|
| Ex20-28 | Appendix | Cost of production report: average cost method | Moderate | Analytic | Process Costing | | Cost Management | Application | 20 min. | | |
| Ex20-29 | Appendix | Cost of production report: average cost method | Moderate | Analytic | Process Costing | | Cost Management | Application | 20 min. | X | |
| Pr20-1A | 20-1, 20-3 | Entries for process cost system | Moderate | Analytic | Process Costing | | Cost Management | Application | 1.5 hours | | X |
| Pr20-2A | 20-2, 20-4 | Cost of production report | Moderate | Analytic | Process Costing | | Cost Management | Application | 1.5 hours | x | |
| Pr20-3A | 20-2, 20-3, 20-4 | Equivalent units and related costs; cost of production report; entries | Challenging | Analytic | Process Costing | | Cost Management | Application | 1.5 hours | x | |
| Pr20-4A | 20-1, 20-2, 20-3 | Work in process account data for two months; cost of production reports | Moderate | Analytic | Process Costing | | Cost Management | Application | 2 hours | X | |
| Pr20-5A | Appendix | Cost of production report: average cost method | Moderate | Analytic | Process Costing | | Cost Management | Application | 1 hour | X | |
| Pr20-1B | 20-1, 20-3 | Entries for process cost system | Moderate | Analytic | Process Costing | | Cost Management | Application | 1.5 hours | | x |
| Pr20-2B | 20-2, 20-4 | Cost of production report | Moderate | Analytic | Process Costing | | Cost Management | Application | 1.5 hours | X | |
| Pr20-3B | 20-2, 20-3, 20-4 | Equivalent units and related costs; cost of production report; entries | Challenging | Analytic | Process Costing | | Cost Management | Application | 1.5 hours | X | |
| Pr20-4B | 20-1, 20-2, 20-3, 20-4 | Work in process account data for two months; cost of production reports | Moderate | Analytic | Process Costing | | Cost Management | Application | 2 hours | X | |
| Pr20-5B | Appendix | Equivalent units and related costs; cost of production report: average cost method | Moderate | Analytic | Process Costing | | Cost Management | Application | 1.5 hours | X | |
| CP20-1 | 20-1 | Ethics and professional conduct in business | Easy | Ethics | Process Costing | | Cost Management | Analysis | 10 min. | | |
| CP20-2 | 20-2 | Accounting for materials costs | Moderate | Analytic | Process Costing | | Cost Management | Analysis | 15 min. | | |
| CP20-3 | 20-4 | Analyzing unit costs | Moderate | Analytic | Process Costing | | Cost Management | Analysis | 15 min. | | |
| CP20-4 | 20-4 | Decision making | Challenging | Analytic | Process Costing | | Cost Management | Analysis | 30 min. | | |
| CP20-5 | 20-1 | Process costing companies | Moderate | Analytic | Process Costing | | Cost Management | Application | 45 min. | | |

# Cost Behavior and Cost-Volume-Profit Analysis

## OPENING COMMENTS

In Chapter 21, students learn how to conduct cost-volume-profit analysis. In preparation for this activity, the chapter discusses variable, fixed, and mixed costs.

Cost-volume-profit analysis is conducted using both a formula-based mathematical approach and a graphic approach. It is applied to single-product and multiple-product companies. The chapter concludes with an appendix that discusses variable costing.

After studying the chapter, your students should be able to:

1.  Classify costs as variable costs, fixed costs, or mixed costs.

2.  Compute the contribution margin, the contribution margin ratio, and the unit contribution margin.

3.  Determine the break-even point and sales necessary to achieve a target profit.

4.  Using a cost-volume-profit chart and a profit-volume chart, determine the break-even point and sales necessary to achieve a target profit.

5.  Compute the break-even point for a company selling more than one product, the operating leverage, and the margin of safety.

# STUDENT FAQS

- Why does variable cost per unit stay the same but total cost varies with the number of units you produce?

- How do you choose what activity base to use?

- Why does fixed cost remain the same in total dollar amount but increase or decrease per unit as the level of activity changes?

- What do increases in fixed cost do to break-even analysis?

- What do increases in variable cost do to break-even analysis?

# OBJECTIVE 1

Classify costs as variable costs, fixed costs, or mixed costs.

## KEY TERMS

| | |
|---|---|
| Activity Bases (Drivers) | Mixed Costs |
| Cost Behavior | Relevant Range |
| Fixed Costs | Variable Costing |
| High-Low Method | Variable Costs |

## SUGGESTED APPROACH

Knowing how costs behave enables management to estimate costs when evaluating alternative operating proposals. Begin your coverage of this objective by reviewing the definitions of variable, fixed, and mixed costs. Be sure to point out the behavior of both total and unit costs. For example, variable costs are illustrated in text Exhibit 1. When reviewing this illustration, stress that as the number of units produced increases, the total direct materials cost increases but the unit cost remains constant.

Fixed costs are shown in text Exhibit 2. This illustration compares the supervisor's salary in a plant that makes perfume to the number of perfume bottles produced. The total salary is constant at all production levels. As a result, the per-unit cost decreases as production increases.

Mixed costs have both a fixed and a variable component. An example of a mixed cost is the price paid to rent a moving van if that price includes a fixed fee plus a charge per mile (i.e., $50 plus $0.30 per mile).

In addition to understanding how costs behave, managers need to know what activities create costs. These activities are called activity bases (or *activity drivers*). Ask your students to identify the activity base that drives their textbook expenditures. (Answer: the number of courses taken)

## GROUP LEARNING ACTIVITY — Variable, Fixed, and Mixed Costs

Divide your class into small groups. Ask them to list examples of fixed, variable, and mixed costs incurred by a McDonald's restaurant. Encourage them to list as many examples as they can. Also instruct them to identify the activity base (driver) for each variable cost on their list.

**Possible response**: McDonald's variable costs could include all the food and drinks, hourly labor, food containers, and condiments. Fixed costs could include rent or mortgage, managers' salaries, insurance, and franchise fees. Mixed costs could include utilities, advertising, and maintenance costs.

## DEMONSTRATION PROBLEM — High-Low Method

For most business analysis, mixed costs must be separated into their fixed and variable components. Use the following problem to demonstrate the high-low method.

The power costs of Jones Manufacturing behave as a mixed cost. The activity that creates most of the power costs is machine usage. Therefore, power costs will be analyzed in relation to machine hours.

Machine hours and power costs for the past six months are presented on Transparency Master (TM) 21-1. Ask students to identify the highest and lowest levels of power usage (August and July respectively). Next, ask them to compute the difference in machine hours and power costs and record these numbers in their notes.

Once the high and low points have been identified, the variable portion of the cost is determined using the following equation:

$$\text{Variable Cost/Unit} = \frac{\text{Difference in Total Cost}}{\text{Difference in Machine Hours}}$$

$$\text{Variable Cost/Unit} = \frac{\$300}{6,000 \text{ hours}} = \$0.05/\text{hour}$$

The fixed portion can be determined using data from either the high or the low power-usage points and the following equation:

$$\text{Total Cost} = (\text{Variable Cost/Unit} \times \text{No. of Units}) + \text{Fixed Costs}$$

Using data from July:

$1,900 = (\$0.05/\text{unit} \times 14,000) + \text{Fixed Costs}$
$1,900 - \$700 = \text{Fixed Costs}$
$1,200 = \text{Fixed Costs}$

# OBJECTIVE 2

**Compute the contribution margin, the contribution margin ratio, and the unit contribution margin.**

## KEY TERMS

Contribution Margin          Cost-Volume-Profit Analysis
Contribution Margin Ratio    Unit Contribution Margin

## SUGGESTED APPROACH

Give students the following formulas related to contribution margin (CM):

CM = Sales – Variable Costs
CM Ratio = CM/Sales

Stress that contribution margin is the amount of funds left from a sale after the variable costs have been paid. Contribution margin is used to pay the fixed costs of the business. Once all fixed costs have been covered, any contribution margin left represents profit.

The contribution margin ratio tells what percent of each sales dollar is contribution margin. Once again, if sales are above break-even, this percentage represents profit.

## GROUP LEARNING ACTIVITY — Contribution Margin

Give your students the following sales and cost data for Van Buren Company. The total sales and cost information is based on the sale of 20,000 units.

|            | Total     | Per Unit |
|------------|-----------|----------|
| Sales      | $570,000  | $28.50   |
| Variable costs | $387,600 | $19.38 |
| Fixed costs | $140,000 |          |

Divide the class into small groups. Ask students to compute the total contribution margin, contribution margin ratio, and unit contribution margin for this company. Also instruct them to compute the increase in net income that will result from a $50,000 increase in sales and a 1,000-unit increase in sales.

The answers to this exercise are as follows:

1. Total contribution margin: $182,400
2. Contribution margin ratio: 32 percent
3. Unit contribution margin: $9.12
4. Increase in net income from $50,000 increase in sales: $50,000 × 32% = $16,000
5. Increase in net income from 1,000-unit increase in sales: 1,000 × $9.12 = $9,120

# OBJECTIVE 3

Determine the break-even point and sales necessary to achieve a target profit.

## KEY TERM

Break-Even Point

## SUGGESTED APPROACH

Under this objective, the text presents formulas to calculate the break-even point in units and the unit sales necessary to achieve a target profit. Use the following lecture notes to explain these formulas.

## LECTURE NOTES — Break-Even Point and Target Profit

Although students generally like to use a "formula" in solving accounting problems, they dislike memorizing them. Remind students that they can use the following formula to solve both break-even and target profit problems as long as they remember that profit is zero at the break-even point.

$$\text{Sales (units)} = \frac{\text{Fixed Costs} + \text{Target Profit}}{\text{Unit Contribution Margin}}$$

Many students benefit from seeing formulas derived from equations they already understand. The text's formula can be derived as follows:

Sales Price (X) – Variable Cost (X) – Fixed Costs = Income from Operations
   where: X = No. of units sold
   also note: sales price and variable cost are per-unit amounts

. . . or (solving for X)
   Sales Price (X) – Variable Cost (X) = Fixed Costs + Income from Operations
   X (Sales Price – Variable Cost) = Fixed Costs + Income from Operations
   X = (Fixed Costs + Income from Operations)/(Sales Price – Variable Cost)
   X = (Fixed Costs + Income from Operations)/Unit Contribution Margin
      Note: "Target profit" is a company's desired income from operations.

In reality, students also can solve break-even and target profit problems using the equation:
Sales Price (X) – Variable Cost (X) – Fixed Costs = Income from Operations. Some of your students will find this equation easiest to remember and use.

## GROUP LEARNING ACTIVITY — Break-Even and Target Profit

One of the true benefits of cost-volume-profit analysis is that a business can analyze a variety of "what-if" scenarios. TM 21-2 presents several what-ifs for your students to answer in small groups. Solutions are presented on TM 21-3.

## WRITING EXERCISE — Break-Even Point

Ask your students to write an answer to the following questions (TM 21-4):

Would an increase in variable costs per unit cause a company's break-even point to increase or decrease? Why?

**Possible response**: An increase in variable costs will cause the break-even point in unit sales to increase. An increase in variable costs leaves less contribution margin to apply toward fixed costs, requiring more units to be sold to cover the fixed costs.

Would an increase in per-unit selling price cause a company's break-even point to increase or decrease? Why?

**Possible response**: An increase in sales price will cause the break-even point in unit sales to decrease. An increased sales price provides additional contribution margin to cover fixed costs, requiring fewer sales to break even.

# OBJECTIVE 4

**Using a cost-volume-profit chart and a profit-volume chart, determine the break-even point and sales necessary to achieve a target profit.**

## KEY TERMS

Cost-Volume-Profit Chart        Profit-Volume Chart

## SUGGESTED APPROACH

The mathematical (formula-based) approach to calculating a break-even point is usually more accurate than the graphic approach. Most students also find the mathematical approach to be a quicker and easier way to solve problems. However, because it is important that students learn how to read business graphs, the graphic approach to break-even analysis deserves attention.

Use Exhibit 5 in the text to review the construction of a cost-volume-profit (CVP) chart. Emphasize that a CVP chart provides a visual representation of the break-even point. The chart consists of a sales line and a cost line. The intersection of these lines is the break-even point.

Exhibit 7 illustrates a profit-volume (PV) chart. A profit line is plotted on a PV chart. The break-even point occurs where the profit line intersects the zero horizontal profit line. This represents the point where profits equal zero.

You may want to focus on the interpretation rather than the preparation of break-even graphs. The group learning activity that follows will ask students to read and interpret cost-volume-profit (CVP) and profit-volume (PV) charts.

## GROUP LEARNING ACTIVITY — CVP and PV Charts

Handout 21-1 presents a CVP chart and a PV chart. It also poses several questions to test your students' ability to read and interpret these graphs. Distribute copies of the handout to your students and ask them to work in small groups to answer the questions.

**Handout 21-1 solutions**:
**Chart 1:** *Question*—See Exhibit 5 in the text for sales and cost line identification; *Question 2*—40,000 units; *Question 3*—$40,000; *Question 4*—Variable cost $.50 per unit [VC = ($60,000 - $40,000)/40,000)]; *Question 5*—profit at 80,000 units is $40,000 [CM × (Unit Sales – Break-Even Units)] OR [($1 × (80,000 – 40,000)]

**Chart 2**: *Question 1*—15,000 units; *Question 2*—$25,000; *Question 3*—$25,000 [CM × (Unit Sales – Break-Even Units)] OR [1.67 × (30,000 – 15,000)]

# OBJECTIVE 5

**Compute the break-even point for a company selling more than one product, the operating leverage, and the margin of safety.**

## KEY TERMS

Margin of Safety          Sales Mix
Operating Leverage

## SUGGESTED APPROACH

Cost-volume-profit analysis can be applied to companies that sell more than one product, as long as their sales mix is constant. Use the Demonstration Problem to illustrate this modification to basic break-even analysis.

Ask your students to identify examples of sales mixes for various real-life businesses. An example would be car dealerships that sell different makes of cars, such as Cadillacs and Buicks.

## DEMONSTRATION PROBLEM — Sales Mix

To calculate the break-even point for a company that sells more than one product, a weighted average contribution margin must be determined. The text illustrates this calculation by multiplying the sales price and then the unit variable cost by the sales mix percentage and adding these two amounts. The calculation can also be performed directly on the unit contribution margin.

For example, assume that a gourmet food manufacturer has considered renting a booth at a local mall to sell gift boxes of candy, nuts, and cookies during the holiday season. The fixed costs to rent and operate the booth would be $27,900. The unit contribution margins and sales mix anticipated by the company are as follows:

|  | Unit Contribution Margin | Sales Mix |
|---|---|---|
| Candy | $1.50 | 50% |
| Nuts | $2.00 | 30% |
| Cookies | $1.00 | 20% |

A weighted average unit contribution margin would be as follows:

$$\$1.50 \times 50\% = \$0.75$$
$$\$2.00 \times 30\% = \ 0.60$$
$$\$1.00 \times 20\% = \underline{\ 0.20}$$
$$\underline{\$1.55}$$

To break even, the company would need to sell 18,000 gift boxes ($27,900/$1.55). Using the sales mix, the number of each type of gift box can be calculated.

$$\text{Candy: } 18,000 \times 50\% = \ 9,000$$
$$\text{Nuts: } \ 18,000 \times 30\% = \ 5,400$$
$$\text{Cookies: } 18,000 \times 20\% = \underline{\ 3,600}$$
$$\underline{18,000}$$

## DEMONSTRATION PROBLEM — Operating Leverage

Operating leverage compares contribution margin to operating income. The formula is:

$$\text{Operating Leverage} = \frac{\text{Contribution Margin}}{\text{Operating Income}}$$

Ask your students to calculate the operating leverage of a company with $800,000 in sales, $200,000 in variable costs, and $400,000 in fixed costs.

$$\text{Operating Leverage} = \$600,000/\$200,000 = 3$$

An operating leverage of 3 indicates that operating income will increase three times any percentage increase in sales. For example, if sales increase 5 percent, operating income will increase 15 percent. You may want to prove this by presenting the follow example.

|  | Original Data | + 5% in Sales |
|---|---|---|
| Sales | $800,000 | $840,000 |
| Variable costs | 200,000 | 210,000 |
| Contribution margin | $600,000 | $630,000 |
| Fixed costs | 400,000 | 400,000 |
| Operating income | $200,000 | $230,000 |

$$\frac{\$30,000}{\$200,000} = 15\% \text{ increase}$$

Stress that large amounts of fixed costs cause companies in capital-intensive industries to have a high operating leverage. Operating leverage is much lower in labor-intensive industries.

## GROUP LEARNING ACTIVITY — Margin of Safety

Explain that margin of safety measures the amount by which current sales exceed sales at the break-even point. It may be expressed in dollars, in units, or as a percentage. When expressed as a percentage, margin of safety shows the percentage that sales can drop without resulting in an operating loss. The formula to calculate margin of safety as a percentage of current sales is as follows:

$$\text{Margin of Safety} = \frac{\text{Sales} - \text{Sales at Break-Even Point}}{\text{Sales}}$$

Ask your students to work in small groups to answer questions related to margin of safety on TM 21-5. The solutions are provided on TM 21-6.

## INTERNET ACTIVITY — Review of Chapter Concepts

CCH Business Owner's Toolkit is an excellent Web site for reviewing cost-volume-profit analysis and related topics from the chapter. Direct your students to the following Web site: http://www.toolkit.cch.com/text/P06_7500.asp

This Web site will present information on using cost-volume-profit analysis in a small business. It also has links to information on breakeven analysis, contribution margin analysis, and operating leverage. The breakeven analysis page includes an interactive calculator that will compute breakeven points and produce a cost-volume-profit graph.

# APPENDIX — VARIABLE COSTING

## KEY TERM

Absorption costing

## SUGGESTED APPROACH

Explain that the name given to the manufacturing cost system your students have been learning is absorption costing. Under absorption costing, all costs necessary to manufacture a product are "absorbed" by the product (included in the product's reported cost). This includes both fixed and variable manufacturing costs. Review absorption costing with the group learning activity that follows.

Explain that variable costing is another approach used for management reporting. Under variable costing, only variable costs are included in the product costs reported as cost of goods sold or ending inventory. All fixed costs are treated as period expenses. The group learning activity and the lecture aids that follow will help you present the basics of variable costing.

## GROUP LEARNING ACTIVITY — Absorption and Variable Costing

To review absorption costing, ask your students to prepare an income statement for Laurens Incorporated, using the data on TM 21-7.

TM 21-8 displays Laurens' income statement under absorption costing. It also shows the company's income statement under variable costing. Point out the $30,000 difference in the two income statements. Ask students to examine the income statements, silently on their own, and look for the reason the statements present a different net income. After a minute, ask them to share their ideas in their group. This group discussion time will allow students to finalize their answers before sharing them with the class.

Through discussion, bring the class to a consensus that the $30,000 difference is the fixed cost of the 2,000 units produced but not sold ($15/unit × 2,000 units). Under full absorption costing, this $30,000 cost is allocated to the units in the ending finished goods inventory. Therefore, it is carried on the balance sheet as an asset. Under variable costing, this $30,000 is reported on the income statement as a period expense. As a result, net income is $30,000 lower under variable costing.

## LECTURE AID — Variable Costing

Although variable costing is not permitted for financial reporting, many managers find it useful for management reporting. Variable costing tends to show costs in the same manner as they are incurred: variable costs on a per-unit basis and fixed costs in total.

Another benefit of variable costing is the ability to isolate the impact of changes in sales or costs. TM 21-9 shows an income statement for Laurens Incorporated, assuming sales of 20,000 units and 30,000 units. Point out that as volume increases, only variable costs change. This is clearly evident from the variable costing income statement.

**Handout 21-1**

### Cost-Volume-Profit Chart

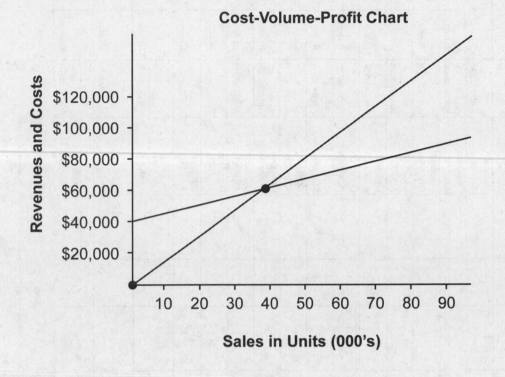

1. Identify the sales and cost lines.
2. What is the break-even point in units?
3. What is the company's total fixed cost?
4. What is the company's variable cost per unit?
5. What is the company's profit at sales of 80,000 units?

### Volume-Profit Chart

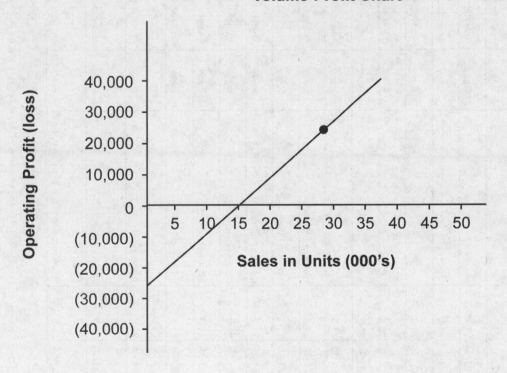

1. What is this company's break-even point in units?
2. What is the company's total fixed cost?
3. What is the company's profit at sales of 30,000 units?

# HOMEWORK CHART WITH LEARNING OUTCOMES TAGGED

| Problem | Learning Objective | Description | DIFFICULTY | BUSPROG Primary | ACBSP Primary | ACBSP Secondary | ACBSP Teritary | ACBSP Quaternary | IMA Managerial Only | BLOOM'S | TIME | Spread-sheet |
|---|---|---|---|---|---|---|---|---|---|---|---|---|
| DQ21-1 | 21-1 | | Easy | Analytic | Variable and Fixed Costs | | | | Cost Management | Knowledge | 5 min. | |
| DQ21-2 | 21-1 | | Easy | Analytic | Variable and Fixed Costs | | | | Cost Management | Knowledge | 5 min. | |
| DQ21-3 | 21-1 | | Easy | Analytic | Variable and Fixed Costs | | | | Cost Management | Knowledge | 5 min. | |
| DQ21-4 | 21-1 | | Easy | Analytic | Variable and Fixed Costs | | | | Cost Management | Knowledge | 5 min. | |
| DQ21-5 | 21-2 | | Easy | Analytic | Variable and Fixed Costs | Contribution Margin | | | Decision Analysis | Knowledge | 5 min. | |
| DQ21-6 | 21-2 | | Easy | Analytic | Contribution Margin | | | | Decision Analysis | Knowledge | 5 min. | |
| DQ21-7 | 21-3 | | Easy | Analytic | Break-even point | | | | Decision Analysis | Knowledge | 5 min. | |
| DQ21-8 | 21-3 | | Easy | Analytic | Break-even point | | | | Decision Analysis | Knowledge | 5 min. | |
| DQ21-9 | 21-5 | | Easy | Analytic | Break-even point | | | | Decision Analysis | Knowledge | 5 min. | |
| DQ21-10 | 21-5 | | Easy | Analytic | Break-even point | | | | Decision Analysis | Knowledge | 5 min. | |
| PE21-1A | 21-1 | High-low method | Easy | Analytic | Variable and Fixed Costs | | | | Cost Management | Application | 10 min. | |
| PE21-1B | 21-1 | High-low method | Easy | Analytic | Variable and Fixed Costs | | | | Cost Management | Application | 10 min. | |
| PE21-2A | 21-2 | Contribution margin | Easy | Analytic | Contribution Margin | | | | Decision Analysis | Application | 10 min. | |
| PE21-2B | 21-2 | Contribution margin | Easy | Analytic | Contribution Margin | | | | Decision Analysis | Application | 10 min. | |
| PE21-3A | 21-3 | Break-even point | Easy | Analytic | Break-even point | | | | Decision Analysis | Application | 10 min. | |
| PE21-3B | 21-3 | Break-even point | Easy | Analytic | Break-even point | | | | Decision Analysis | Application | 10 min. | |
| PE21-4A | 21-3 | Target profit | Easy | Analytic | Margin of safety/sales target | | | | Decision Analysis | Application | 10 min. | |
| PE21-4B | 21-3 | Target profit | Easy | Analytic | Margin of safety/sales target | | | | Decision Analysis | Application | 10 min. | |
| PE21-5A | 21-5 | Sales mix and break-even analysis | Easy | Analytic | Margin of safety/sales target | | | | Decision Analysis | Application | 10 min. | |

| Problem | Learning Objective | Description | DIFFICULTY | BUSPROG Primary | ACBSP Primary | ACBSP Secondary | ACBSP Tertiary | ACBSP Quaternary | IMA Managerial Only | BLOOM'S | TIME | Spread-sheet |
|---|---|---|---|---|---|---|---|---|---|---|---|---|
| PE21-5B | 21-5 | Sales mix and break-even analysis | Easy | Analytic | Margin of safety/sales target | Break-even point | | | Decision Analysis | Application | 10 min. | |
| PE21-6A | 21-5 | Operating leverage | Easy | Analytic | CVP Analysis | | | | Decision Analysis | Application | 5 min. | |
| PE21-6B | 21-5 | Operating leverage | Easy | Analytic | CVP Analysis | | | | Decision Analysis | Application | 5 min. | |
| PE21-7A | 21-5 | Margin of safety | Easy | Analytic | Margin of safety/sales target | | | | Decision Analysis | Application | 5 min. | |
| PE21-7B | 21-5 | Margin of safety | Easy | Analytic | Margin of safety/sales target | | | | Decision Analysis | Application | 5 min. | |
| Ex21-1 | 21-1 | Classify costs | Easy | Analytic | Variable and Fixed Costs | | | | Decision Analysis | Knowledge | 15 min. | |
| Ex21-2 | 21-1 | Identify cost graphs | Easy | Analytic | CVP Analysis | | | | Decision Analysis | Application | 15 min. | |
| Ex21-3 | 21-1 | Identify activity bases | Easy | Analytic | Managerial Accounting Features/Costs | | | | Cost Management | Knowledge | 15 min. | |
| Ex21-4 | 21-1 | Identify activity bases | Easy | Analytic | Managerial Accounting Features/Costs | | | | Cost Management | Knowledge | 15 min. | |
| Ex21-5 | 21-1 | Identify fixed and variable costs | Easy | Analytic | Variable and Fixed Costs | | | | Cost Management | Knowledge | 15 min. | |
| Ex21-6 | 21-1 | Relevant range and fixed and variable costs | Moderate | Analytic | Variable and Fixed Costs | | | | Cost Management | Application | 20 min. | |
| Ex21-7 | 21-1 | High-low method | Easy | Analytic | Variable and Fixed Costs | | | | Cost Management | Application | 15 min. | X |
| Ex21-8 | 21-1 | High-low method for service company | Moderate | Analytic | Variable and Fixed Costs | | | | Cost Management | Application | 20 min. | |
| Ex21-9 | 21-2 | Contribution margin ratio | Easy | Analytic | Contribution Margin | | | | Decision Analysis | Application | 10 min. | |
| Ex21-10 | 21-2 | Contribution margin and contribution margin ratio | Moderate | Analytic | Break-even point | | | | Decision Analysis | Application | 15 min. | |
| Ex21-11 | 21-3 | Break-even sales and sales to realize income from operations | Easy | Analytic | Break-even point | | | | Decision Analysis | Application | 10 min. | |
| Ex21-12 | 21-3 | Break-even sales | Moderate | Analytic | Break-even point | | | | Decision Analysis | Application | 15 min. | |
| Ex21-13 | 21-3 | Break-even sales | Easy | Analytic | Break-even point | | | | Decision Analysis | Application | 10 min. | |
| Ex21-14 | 21-3 | Break-even analysis | Easy | Analytic | Break-even point | | | | Decision Analysis | Application | 10 min. | |

| Problem | Learning Objective | Description | DIFFICULTY | BUSPROG Primary | ACBSP Primary | ACBSP Secondary | ACBSP Teritary | ACBSP Quaternary | IMA Managerial Only | BLOOM'S | TIME | Spreadsheet |
|---|---|---|---|---|---|---|---|---|---|---|---|---|
| Ex21-15 | 21-3 | Break-even analysis | Moderate | Analytic | Break-even point | | | | Decision Analysis | Application | 15 min. | |
| Ex21-16 | 21-3 | Break-even analysis | Moderate | Analytic | Break-even point | | | | Decision Analysis | Application | 15 min. | X |
| Ex21-17 | 21-4 | Cost-volume-profit chart | Moderate | Analytic | CVP Analysis | | | | Decision Analysis | Application | 20 min. | |
| Ex21-18 | 21-4 | Profit-volume chart | Moderate | Analytic | CVP Analysis | | | | Decision Analysis | Application | 20 min. | |
| Ex21-19 | 21-4 | Break-even chart | Moderate | Analytic | Break-even point | | | | Decision Analysis | Application | 15 min. | |
| Ex21-20 | 21-4 | Break-even chart | Moderate | Analytic | Break-even point | Margin of safety/sales target | | | Decision Analysis | Application | 15 min. | |
| Ex21-21 | 21-5 | Sales mix and break-even sales | Moderate | Analytic | Break-even point | Margin of safety/sales target | | | Decision Analysis | Application | 15 min. | |
| Ex21-22 | 21-5 | Break-even sales and sales mix for a service company | Moderate | Analytic | Break-even point | | | | Decision Analysis | Application | 20 min. | |
| Ex21-23 | 21-5 | Margin of safety | Moderate | Analytic | Margin of safety/sales target | | | | Decision Analysis | Application | 15 min. | |
| Ex21-24 | 21-5 | Break-even and margin of safety relationships | Moderate | Analytic | Margin of safety/sales target | | | | Decision Analysis | Application | 10 min. | |
| Ex21-25 | 21-5 | Operating leverage | Moderate | Analytic | CVP Analysis | | | | Decision Analysis | Application | 15 min. | |
| Ex21-26 | Appendix | Items on variable costing income statement | Easy | Analytic | CVP Analysis | | | | Decision Analysis | Application | 5 min. | |
| Ex21-27 | Appendix | Variable costing income statement | Moderate | Analytic | CVP Analysis | CVP Analysis | | | Decision Analysis | Application | 15 min. | X |
| Ex21-28 | Appendix | Absorption costing income statement | Moderate | Analytic | CVP Analysis | CVP Analysis | | | Decision Analysis | Application | 20 min. | X |
| Pr21-1A | 21-1 | Classify costs | Moderate | Analytic | Variable and Fixed Costs | | | | Cost Management | Application | 45 min | |
| Pr21-2A | 21-2, 21-3 | Break-even sales under present and proposed conditions | Challenging | Analytic | Break-even point | | | | Decision Analysis | Application | 2 hours | |
| Pr21-3A | 21-3, 21-4 | Break-even sales and cost-volume-profit chart | Moderate | Analytic | Break-even point | CVP Analysis | | | Decision Analysis | Application | 1 hour | |
| Pr21-4A | 21-3, 21-4 | Break-even sales and cost-volume-profit chart | Challenging | Analytic | Break-even point | CVP Analysis | | | Decision Analysis | Application | 1.5 hours | |
| Pr21-5A | 21-5 | Sales mix and break-even sales | Moderate | Analytic | Break-even point | Margin of safety/sales target | | | Decision Analysis | Application | 1.5 hours | |

| Problem | Learning Objective | Description | DIFFICULTY | BUSPROG Primary | ACBSP Primary | ACBSP Secondary | ACBSP Tertiary | ACBSP Quaternary | IMA Managerial Only | BLOOM'S | TIME | Spreadsheet |
|---|---|---|---|---|---|---|---|---|---|---|---|---|
| Pr21-6A | 21-2, 21-3, 21-4, 21-5 | Contribution margin, break-even sales, cost-volume-profit chart, margin of safety, and operating leverage | Challenging | Analytic | Contribution Margin | Break-even point | CVP Analysis | Margin of safety/sales target | Decision Analysis | Application | 1.5 hours | X |
| Pr21-1B | 21-1 | Classify costs | Moderate | Analytic | Variable and Fixed Costs | | | | Decision Analysis | Application | 45 min. | |
| Pr21-2B | 21-2, 21-3 | Break-even sales under present and proposed conditions | Challenging | Analytic | Break-even point | | | | Decision Analysis | Application | 2 hours | |
| Pr21-3B | 21-3, 21-4 | Break-even sales and cost-volume-profit chart | Moderate | Analytic | Break-even point | CVP Analysis | | | Decision Analysis | Application | 1 hour | |
| Pr21-4B | 21-3, 21-4 | Break-even sales and cost-volume-profit chart | Challenging | Analytic | Break-even point | CVP Analysis | | | Decision Analysis | Application | 1.5 hours | |
| Pr21-5B | 21-5 | Sales mix and break-even sales | Moderate | Analytic | Break-even point | Margin of safety/sales target | | | Decision Analysis | Application | 1.5 hours | |
| Pr21-6B | 21-2, 21-3, 21-4, 21-5 | Contribution margin, break-even sales, cost-volume-profit chart, margin of safety, and operating leverage | Challenging | Analytic | Contribution Margin | Break-even point | CVP Analysis | Margin of safety/sales target | Decision Analysis | Application | 1.5 hours | X |
| CP21-1 | 21-3 | Ethics and professional conduct in business | Moderate | Ethics | Break-even point | | | | Ethical Considerations | Analysis | 15 min. | |
| CP21-2 | 21-2, 21-3 | Break-even sales, contribution margin | Moderate | Analytic | Break-even point | Contribution Margin | | | Decision Analysis | Comprehension | 15 min. | |
| CP21-3 | 21-3 | Break-even analysis | Moderate | Analytic | Break-even point | | | | Decision Analysis | Analysis | 15 min. | |
| CP21-4 | 21-3, 21-4 | Variable costs and activity bases in decision making | Moderate | Analytic | Variable and Fixed Costs | | | | Cost Management | Analysis | 30 min. | |
| CP21-5 | 21-3, 21-4 | Variable costs and activity bases in decision making | Challenging | Analytic | Variable and Fixed Costs | | | | Cost Management | Analysis | 30 min. | |
| CP21-6 | 21-3 | Break-even analysis | Moderate | Analytic | Break-even point | | | | Decision Analysis | Application | 1 hour | |

# Budgeting

## OPENING COMMENTS

Chapter 22 emphasizes accounting activities that help managers plan, direct, and control the operations of a business. Budgeting is used to establish business goals in the planning function. Budgets help guide managers' operational decisions. Budgets are also used to control operations as actual results are compared to the budgeted results.

After studying the chapter, your students should be able to:

1. Describe budgeting, its objectives, and its impact on human behavior.

2. Describe the basic elements of the budget process, the two major types of budgeting, and the use of computers in budgeting.

3. Describe the master budget for a manufacturing company.

4. Prepare the basic income statement budgets for a manufacturing company.

5. Prepare balance sheet budgets for a manufacturing company.

## STUDENT FAQS

- Since budgets are estimates made before a period begins and may prove wrong, are they worth the time and effort put into them?

- Why are the cash budget and the capital expenditures budget so important from the balance sheet budgeting process?

- In a production budget, the volume of production is the first thing to calculate, but deducting the estimated units in beginning inventory and adding the desired units in ending inventory seems opposite. Can you explain so I can understand better?

- How do you calculate manufacturing cost?

- The cost of goods sold budget is so long. Why do you expect us to learn to calculate it without the formula written out?

# OBJECTIVE 1

**Describe budgeting, its objectives, and its impact on human behavior.**

## KEY TERMS

Budgets                          Goal Conflict
Budgetary Slack            Responsibility Center

## SUGGESTED APPROACH

A budget is used to plan and control operational departments and divisions. Review this explanation and stress the following points:

1. Budgeting begins with *planning,* which involves setting specific goals for future operations.
2. *Directing* involves decisions and actions to achieve the budgeted goals.
3. *Controlling* is periodically comparing actual results to these goals.
4. Budgets are most effective if:
   a. Employees help set goals they are expected to achieve.
   b. Budgets are realistic, not too strict.
   c. Budgets are not "padded" or too loose.
   d. Budgets do not encourage employees to act in ways that conflict with business goals.

An example of goal conflict can be taken from the way many instructors assign course grades. There may be a conflict if the instructor wants students to participate in class discussions, but bases course grades strictly on exam scores.

## CLASS DISCUSSION — Human Behavior and Budgeting

Ask your students to share examples from their own experiences where budgets caused employees to act in a manner that hurt the performance or profitability of their organization. After accumulating your students' ideas, add observations from your own experience. For example, there is usually no incentive for managers to spend less than their allowed budget, since it will be difficult to negotiate a higher budget the next year. As a result, managers frequently "spend the budget" as the fiscal year closes.

## WRITING EXERCISE — Evaluating Budgeting Procedures

Ask your students to write an answer to the following question (Transparency Master [TM] 22-1).

Pretorious Manufacturing has just hired a new controller, Diana Metcalf. During her first week on the job, Diana was asked to establish a budget for operating expenses in 2014. Since Diana was not yet familiar with the operations of Pretorious Manufacturing, she decided to budget these expenses using the same procedures as the prior controller. Therefore, in order to establish a budget for operating expenses, Diana started with actual operating expenses incurred in 2013 and added 4.3 percent. Diana based this percentage on inflation as measured by the consumer price index.

Comment on the effectiveness of Diana's budgeting strategy.

**Possible response**: This method of budgeting would be the least desirable method. Although the previous year's budget is a starting point, additional input is required to validate that budget to determine if changes need to be made. Proper budgeting procedures require the input of various key management employees in order to accurately predict the company's needs for the approaching financial period. This process should be coordinated by a budgeting committee that gathers information about sales, purchases, capital needs, personnel needs, and various other operational needs. This input will be used to develop the budget for the impending financial period.

## INTERNET ACTIVITY — Personal Budgeting

To spark interest in the topic of budgeting, ask your students to do a Web search using the word "Budgeting" as the search criteria. This search should find a variety of Web sites with information on preparing a personal budget. Ask your students to find a couple of tips on developing a personal budget to share with the class.

# OBJECTIVE 2

**Describe the basic elements of the budget process, the two major types of budgeting, and the use of computers in budgeting.**

## KEY TERMS

Continuous Budgeting          Static Budget
Flexible Budget                     Zero-Based Budgeting

## SUGGESTED APPROACH

TM 22-2 describes the two major types of budgets, the static budget and the flexible budget. When covering zero-based budgeting, point out that it is rare for an organization to require zero-based budgeting every year. More typically, zero-based budgeting is used as a tool to take a fresh view of operations each year. Also point out that the more common approach to budgeting is to start with the prior year's budget and revise it to reflect changes that are expected in the coming year. Static budgeting is used mostly for administrative, selling, and overhead departments. A production department would use flexible budgeting.

Follow this introduction with additional material to reinforce the concept of a flexible budget. A thorough understanding of flexible budgeting is essential to material presented in this chapter and Chapter 23, which addresses standard costing.

## WRITING EXERCISE — Flexible Budgets

As an introduction to flexible budgets, ask your students to write a response to the following question (TM 22-3).

> Assume that you manage one store in a chain of sporting goods retailers. Each month, your store is evaluated by comparing actual operating results to budgeted results.
>
> During December of the current year, your store's sales were up 25 percent from sales projected on the budget. As a result of this increase in sales, would you expect any other items to come in over (or under) their budgeted amounts? If so, list the items and describe why they would vary from the budget.

**Possible response:** Items that would be affected by sales higher than budgeted might include cost of merchandise sold, sales commissions, and other selling expenses. Flexible budgeting at various sales levels could address this situation.

## DEMONSTRATION PROBLEM — Benefits of Flexible Budgeting

As an alternative to the writing exercise above, you may want to capture your students' attention by demonstrating the ineffectiveness of a static budget. Relate a static budget to a student's personal budget. Assume the student budgets $30 per month for gas. However, during the year, the student gets a job delivering pizza. As a result, the student spends more than the budget because of increased gas expenses. Is this really "bad news"? Not if the student's wages and tips exceed the additional expenses.

TM 22-4 presents information for the Laboratory Services department of Eastgate Hospital. On this TM, a static budget is compared to actual results. Ask students to comment on how actual results compared to the hospital's budget. They will quickly point out that the department was $50,000 over budget. Next, ask students to evaluate why the variance occurred or to comment on the efficiency of operations. It will be impossible for them to make any meaningful conclusions from the limited data given.

Next, show TM 22-5, which presents actual results compared against a flexible budget at two activity levels. Ask students to evaluate the performance of the Laboratory Services department, using this information. They will be able to see that the department performed quite well, given the increase in actual test volume. The department actually spent less than what would be expected for performing 14,800 tests. The flexible budget is much more useful than the static budget for planning and control.

## LECTURE AID — Preparing a Flexible Budget

By definition, variable costs increase as sales or production increases. Flexible budgets allow a company to budget for varying levels of sales and production.  The following steps are used in preparing a flexible budget.

1.  Identify the relevant activity levels.
2.  Identify the fixed and variable cost components of the costs being budgeted.
3.  Prepare the budget for each activity level then add the fixed cost for the period.

## GROUP LEARNING ACTIVITY — Flexible Budget

TM 22-6 provides information to be used to complete a flexible budget for a manufacturer. Divide your class into small groups and ask them to prepare the budget for the indicated levels. Recalculating the budget for three activity levels will emphasize the usefulness of computers in preparing budgets. You may want to mention that computer software systems such as spreadsheets and integrated budget and planning programs ease the budget preparation process as well as serve to provide timely results for analysis. The correct solution is listed on TM 22-7.

# OBJECTIVE 3
**Describe the master budget for a manufacturing company.**

## KEY TERM

Master Budget

## SUGGESTED APPROACH

The master budget is the comprehensive budget plan that includes the many individual budgets used to estimate income statement and balance sheet items. These budgets are listed in the text under Objective 3. The actual preparation of the components of the master budget is covered under Objectives 4 and 5.

Refer your students to Exhibit 7 in the text. This exhibit diagrams the relationship between the income statement budgets within the master budget. Use this illustration to emphasize the importance of properly organizing the budgeting process. Also stress the dramatic affect budgeting errors can have as they "ripple down" through the organization.

You may also want to obtain a copy of your college or university budget and distribute it in class as an example of a master budget. The budgets of most state agencies are public information.

# OBJECTIVE 4

Prepare the basic income statement budgets for a manufacturing company.

## KEY TERMS

Cost of Goods Sold Budget

Direct Labor Cost Budget

Direct Materials Purchases Budget

Factory Overhead Cost Budget

Production Budget

Sales Budget

## SUGGESTED APPROACH

The budgets prepared by a manufacturer related to income statement items include:

1. Sales budget
2. Production budget
3. Direct materials purchases budget
4. Direct labor cost budget
5. Factory overhead cost budget
6. Cost of goods sold budget
7. Selling and administrative expenses budget
8. Budgeted income statement

It is difficult (if not impossible) to demonstrate all of these budgets in class. Therefore, you may want to restrict class coverage to the more complicated budgets: production, direct materials purchases, and cost of goods sold.

Do take the time to emphasize the importance of the sales budget. An accurate sales budget is critical, since other budgets depend upon the planned level of sales.

## DEMONSTRATION PROBLEM — Production Budget

The basic format of a production budget is as follows:

|   | Expected Sales in Units |
| --- | --- |
| + | Desired Units in Ending Inventory |
| = | Total Units Needed |
| − | Estimated Units in Beginning Inventory |
|   | Total Units to be Produced |

Explain that the ending inventory provides a cushion in case sales exceed projections or production falls short of the budget. It also gives the company units to sell at the beginning of the following budget period.

Demonstrate this budget using the following information:

Miles Manufacturing has prepared the following sales budget for the first four months of the year:

| | January | February | March | April |
|---|---|---|---|---|
| Sales | 20,000 | 22,000 | 25,000 | 21,000 |

Miles estimates that it will begin the year with 3,000 units in inventory. The company wants to end each month with inventory equal to 25 percent of the next month's projected sales. Prepare a production budget for January through March.

| | January | February | March |
|---|---|---|---|
| Expected Sales in Units | 20,000 | 22,000 | 25,000 |
| Desired Units for Ending Inventory | 5,500 | 6,250 | 5,250 |
| Total Units Needed | 25,500 | 28,250 | 30,250 |
| Estimated Units in Beg. Inventory | 3,000 | 5,500 | 6,250 |
| Total Units to be Produced | 22,500 | 22,750 | 24,000 |

Note that the ending inventory of one month becomes the beginning inventory of the following month.

## GROUP LEARNING ACTIVITY — Direct Materials Purchases Budget

The direct materials purchases budget follows the same basic format as the production budget. The only modification is that this budget must be prepared in both units and dollars because the cost of materials purchased is used in the cost of goods sold budget.

The direct materials purchases budget is prepared as follows:

| | |
|---|---|
| | Materials Required for Production |
| + | Desired Ending Materials Inventory |
| − | Estimated Beginning Materials Inventory |
| = | Direct Materials to Be Purchased |
| × | Unit Price |
| = | Total Direct Materials Purchases |

Divide your class into small groups. Ask students to prepare a direct materials purchases budget for Miles Manufacturing for January and February, using their notes from the preceding demonstration problem and the following additional information:

1. Each unit requires two pounds of materials.
2. Materials cost $0.60 per pound.
3. Miles estimates that it will have 4,000 pounds of materials inventory on January 1.
4. Miles' desired ending inventory for materials is 5,000 pounds.

The solution to this activity is presented on TM 22-8.

## LECTURE AID — Direct Labor and Overhead Budgets

Because the direct labor and overhead budgets are used in the cost of goods sold budget, you may want to quickly review their format.

The direct labor cost budget is prepared as follows:

$$
\begin{array}{rl}
 & \text{Units to Be Produced (from production budget)} \\
\times & \underline{\text{Hours Required per Unit}} \\
= & \text{Total Hours Required for Production} \\
\times & \underline{\text{Hourly Rate}} \\
= & \text{Total Direct Labor Cost}
\end{array}
$$

A direct labor budget is illustrated in text Exhibit 11. Emphasize that the production and direct labor budgets must be closely coordinated. If a failure to properly budget labor time results in a labor shortage, the business may be forced to pay significant amounts of overtime, delay production, or use untrained workers whose output is poor in quality.

To prepare an overhead budget, expected overhead costs are listed and totaled. Exhibit 12 illustrates an overhead budget. Point out that real-world organizations normally have detailed schedules to support each item presented on an overhead budget.

## GROUP LEARNING ACTIVITY — Cost of Goods Sold Budget

The cost of goods sold budget is complex enough to merit a brief explanation plus an in-class practice problem. Use TM 22-9 to review the basic format of the cost of goods sold budget. This TM emphasizes that the budget combines the calculation of three amounts: (1) total manufacturing costs, (2) cost of goods manufactured, and (3) cost of goods sold. Keep in mind that since this edition of the textbook emphasizes the perpetual inventory system, your students will not have practiced calculating cost of goods sold. They also have not previously seen the cost of goods manufactured statement.

While reviewing TM 22-9, stress the sources for the following information:

| Information | Source |
|---|---|
| Beginning Finished Goods Inventory | Management's estimate |
| Beginning Work in Process Inventory | Management's estimate |
| Beginning Direct Materials Inventory | Direct materials purchases budget (no. of units × unit price) |
| Direct Materials Purchases | Direct materials purchases budget |
| Ending Direct Materials Inventory | Direct materials purchases budget (no. of units × unit price) |
| Direct Labor | Direct labor cost budget |
| Factory Overhead | Factory overhead cost budget |
| Ending Work in Process Inventory | Management's desired ending inventory |
| Ending Finished Goods Inventory | Management's desired ending inventory |

Handout 22-1 presents information that your students can use to practice preparing a cost of goods sold budget. Ask them to complete this budget as a group activity. The solution is displayed on TM 22-10.

# OBJECTIVE 5

**Prepare balance sheet budgets for a manufacturing company.**

## KEY TERMS

Capital Expenditures Budget     Cash Budget

## SUGGESTED APPROACH

The two balance sheet budgets presented under this objective are the cash budget and the capital expenditures budget. The capital expenditures budget, which summarizes plans for acquiring fixed assets, is illustrated in Exhibit 19 in the text. Refer your students to this illustration. Emphasize that most companies budget capital expenditures for several years into the future, due to the large dollar amounts associated with these expenditures and the variation in need for capital improvements from year to year.

The cash budget is very important because managers must effectively manage cash to maintain a favorable credit rating, keep borrowing costs to a minimum, and maximize investment income. A sample cash budget is illustrated in text Exhibit 18. Review the basic outline of the cash budget using TM 22-11. Emphasize that the final line of the budget (excess or deficiency) allows companies to gauge whether they will need to arrange for a line of credit to meet cash shortages or whether they will have excess cash to invest. Next, use the group learning activities below to guide students through the calculation of cash receipts and cash payments.

## GROUP LEARNING ACTIVITY — Cash Receipts

The portion of the cash budget that tends to be the most difficult for students is determining the cash receipts from sales. The difficulty occurs because credit sales are frequently collected over two or more months.

TM 22-12 presents information for your students to use in preparing the cash receipts portion of a cash budget. This TM contains data and a basic "shell" format for determining the collections on credit sales. Divide the class into groups and ask them to complete this exercise. TM 22-13 shows the correct solution.

## GROUP LEARNING ACTIVITY — Cash Payments

TMs 22-14 and 22-15 present an opportunity for your students to practice preparing a schedule of cash payments. Prior to assigning this activity, remind students that financial accounting recognizes expenses when they are incurred, not when they are paid. A cash budget reports expenses in the month they are paid. The solution to this exercise is shown on TM 22-16.

**Handout 22-1**

# Cost of Goods Sold Budget

The following are the direct materials purchases, direct labor cost, and factory overhead budgets for Bowerman Corporation for the month of August.

## Direct Materials Purchases Budget

|  | Material A | Material B |
|---|---|---|
| Units required for production | 20,000 | 14,000 |
| Plus desired ending inventory | 8,000 | 2,500 |
| Total | 28,000 | 16,500 |
| Less estimated beginning inventory | 7,400 | 3,000 |
| Units to be purchased | 20,600 | 13,500 |
| Unit price | × $0.50 | × $1.20 |
| Total direct materials purchases | $10,300 | $16,200 |

## Direct Labor Cost Budget

| | |
|---|---|
| Hours required for production | 5,000 |
| Hourly rate | × $10 |
| Total direct labor cost | $50,000 |

## Factory Overhead Cost Budget

| | |
|---|---|
| Supervisor salaries | $18,000 |
| Utilities | 3,500 |
| Depreciation | 7,400 |
| Indirect materials | 2,100 |
| Total factory overhead cost | $31,000 |

Bowerman also estimates the following beginning and ending inventory amounts.

|  | Beginning Inventory | Ending Inventory |
|---|---|---|
| Work in Process | $35,000 | $30,000 |
| Finished Goods | 87,000 | 90,000 |

Required: Prepare a cost of goods sold budget for Bowerman Corporation.

# HOMEWORK CHART WITH LEARNING OUTCOMES TAGGING

| Problem | Learning Objective | Description | DIFFICULTY | BUSPROG Primary | ACBSP Primary | IMA Managerial Only | BLOOM'S | TIME | Spread-sheet |
|---|---|---|---|---|---|---|---|---|---|
| DQ22-1 | 22-1 | | Easy | Analytic | Budgeting and Responsibility | Budget Preparation | Knowledge | 5 min. | |
| DQ22-2 | 22-1 | | Easy | Analytic | Budgeting and Responsibility | Budget Preparation | Knowledge | 5 min. | |
| DQ22-3 | 22-1 | | Easy | Analytic | Budgeting and Responsibility | Budget Preparation | Knowledge | 5 min. | |
| DQ22-4 | 22-1 | | Easy | Analytic | Budgeting and Responsibility | Budget Preparation | Knowledge | 5 min. | |
| DQ22-5 | 22-2 | | Easy | Analytic | Budgeting and Responsibility | Budget Preparation | Knowledge | 5 min. | |
| DQ22-6 | 22-2 | | Easy | Analytic | Budgeting and Responsibility | Budget Preparation | Knowledge | 5 min. | |
| DQ22-7 | 22-4 | | Easy | Analytic | Budgeting and Responsibility | Budget Preparation | Knowledge | 5 min. | |
| DQ22-8 | 22-4 | | Easy | Analytic | Budgeting and Responsibility | Budget Preparation | Knowledge | 5 min. | |
| DQ22-9 | 22-5 | | Easy | Analytic | Budgeting and Responsibility | Budget Preparation | Knowledge | 5 min. | |
| DQ22-10 | 22-5 | | Easy | Analytic | Budgeting and Responsibility | Budget Preparation | Knowledge | 5 min. | |
| PE22-1A | 22-2 | Flexible budgeting | Easy | Analytic | Budgeting and Responsibility | Budget Preparation | Application | 5 min. | |
| PE22-1B | 22-2 | Flexible budgeting | Easy | Analytic | Budgeting and Responsibility | Budget Preparation | Application | 5 min. | |
| PE22-2A | 22-4 | Production budget | Easy | Analytic | Budgeting and Responsibility | Budget Preparation | Application | 5 min. | |
| PE22-2B | 22-4 | Production budget | Easy | Analytic | Budgeting and Responsibility | Budget Preparation | Application | 5 min. | |
| PE22-3A | 22-4 | Direct materials purchases budget | Easy | Analytic | Budgeting and Responsibility | Budget Preparation | Application | 5 min. | |
| PE22-3B | 22-4 | Direct material purchases budget | Easy | Analytic | Budgeting and Responsibility | Budget Preparation | Application | 5 min. | |
| PE22-4A | 22-4 | Direct labor cost budget | Easy | Analytic | Budgeting and Responsibility | Budget Preparation | Application | 5 min. | |
| PE22-4B | 22-4 | Direct labor cost budget | Easy | Analytic | Budgeting and Responsibility | Budget Preparation | Application | 5 min. | |
| PE22-5A | 22-4 | Cost of goods sold budget | Easy | Analytic | Budgeting and Responsibility | Budget Preparation | Application | 10 min. | |
| PE22-5B | 22-4 | Cost of goods sold budget | Easy | Analytic | Budgeting and Responsibility | Budget Preparation | Application | 10 min. | |
| PE22-6A | 22-5 | Cash budget | Easy | Analytic | Budgeting and Responsibility | Budget Preparation | Application | 5 min. | |
| PE22-6B | 22-5 | Cash budget | Easy | Analytic | Budgeting and Responsibility | Budget Preparation | Application | 5 min. | |
| Ex22-1 | 22-2, 22-5 | Personal budget | Easy | Analytic | Budgeting and Responsibility | Budget Preparation | Application | 15 min. | X |
| Ex22-2 | 22-2, 22-4 | Flexible budget for selling and administrative expenses | Easy | Analytic | Budgeting and Responsibility | Budget Preparation | Application | 20 min. | x |
| Ex22-3 | 22-2, 22-4 | Static budget vs. flexible budget | Easy | Analytic | Budgeting and Responsibility | Budget Preparation | Application | 20 min. | X |
| Ex22-4 | 22-2 | Flexible budget for Fabrication Department | Easy | Analytic | Budgeting and Responsibility | Budget Preparation | Application | 15 min. | X |
| Ex22-5 | 22-4 | Production Budget | Easy | Analytic | Budgeting and Responsibility | Budget Preparation | Application | 15 min. | |
| Ex22-6 | 22-4 | Sales and production budgets | Easy | Analytic | Budgeting and Responsibility | Budget Preparation | Application | 20 min. | X |
| Ex22-7 | 22-4 | Professional fees earned budget | Easy | Analytic | Budgeting and Responsibility | Budget Preparation | Application | 10 min. | |
| Ex22-8 | 22-4 | Professional labor cost budget | Easy | Analytic | Budgeting and Responsibility | Budget Preparation | Application | 10 min. | |
| Ex22-9 | 22-4 | Direct materials purchases budget | Moderate | Analytic | Budgeting and Responsibility | Budget Preparation | Application | 20 min. | X |
| Ex22-10 | 22-4 | Direct materials purchases budget | Moderate | Analytic | Budgeting and Responsibility | Budget Preparation | Application | 20 min. | |

| Problem | Learning Objective | Description | DIFFICULTY | BUSPROG Primary | ACBSP Primary | IMA Managerial Only | BLOOM'S | TIME | Spreadsheet |
|---|---|---|---|---|---|---|---|---|---|
| Ex22-11 | 22-4 | Direct materials purchases budget | Moderate | Analytic | Budgeting and Responsibility | Budget Preparation | Application | 20 min. | X |
| Ex22-12 | 22-4 | Direct labor cost budget | Moderate | Analytic | Budgeting and Responsibility | Budget Preparation | Application | 20 min. | |
| Ex22-13 | 22-4 | Direct labor budget-service business budgets | Moderate | Analytic | Budgeting and Responsibility | Budget Preparation | Application | 20 min. | X |
| Ex22-14 | 22-4 | Factory overhead cost budget | Moderate | Analytic | Budgeting and Responsibility | Budget Preparation | Application | 30 min. | X |
| Ex22-15 | 22-4 | Cost of goods sold budget | Moderate | Analytic | Budgeting and Responsibility | Budget Preparation | Application | 20 min. | X |
| Ex22-16 | 22-4 | Cost of goods sold budget | Moderate | Analytic | Budgeting and Responsibility | Budget Preparation | Application | 20 min. | X |
| Ex22-17 | 22-4 | Cost of goods sold budget | Challenging | Analytic | Budgeting and Responsibility | Budget Preparation | Application | 30 min. | |
| Ex22-18 | 22-5 | Schedule of cash collections of accounts receivable | Easy | Analytic | Budgeting and Responsibility | Budget Preparation | Application | 15 min. | X |
| Ex22-19 | 22-5 | Schedule of cash collections of accounts receivable | Easy | Analytic | Budgeting and Responsibility | Budget Preparation | Application | 15 min. | |
| Ex22-20 | 22-5 | Schedule of cash payments | Easy | Analytic | Budgeting and Responsibility | Budget Preparation | Application | 15 min. | |
| Ex22-21 | 22-5 | Schedule of cash payments | Moderate | Analytic | Budgeting and Responsibility | Budget Preparation | Application | 20 min. | X |
| Ex22-22 | 22-5 | Capital expenditures budget | Challenging | Analytic | Budgeting and Responsibility | Budget Preparation | Application | 30 min. | X |
| Pr22-1A | 22-4 | Forecast sales volume and sales budget | Moderate | Analytic | Budgeting and Responsibility | Budget Preparation | Application | 1.5 hours | X |
| Pr22-2A | 22-4 | Sales, production, direct materials purchases, and direct labor cost budgets | Moderate | Analytic | Budgeting and Responsibility | Budget Preparation | Application | 2 hours | X |
| Pr22-3A | 22-4 | Budgeted income statement and supporting budgets | Challenging | Analytic | Budgeting and Responsibility | Budget Preparation | Application | 2.5 hours | X |
| Pr22-4A | 22-5 | Cash budget | Challenging | Analytic | Budgeting and Responsibility | Budget Preparation | Application | 2 hours | X |
| Pr22-5A | 22-4, 22-5 | Budgeted income statement and balance sheet | Challenging | Analytic | Budgeting and Responsibility | Budget Preparation | Application | 2 hours | X |
| Pr22-1B | 22-4 | Forecast sales volume and sales budget | Moderate | Analytic | Budgeting and Responsibility | Budget Preparation | Application | 1.5 hours | X |
| Pr22-2B | 22-4 | Sales, production, direct materials purchases, and direct labor cost budgets | Moderate | Analytic | Budgeting and Responsibility | Budget Preparation | Application | 2 hours | X |
| Pr22-3B | 22-4 | Budgeted income statement and supporting budgets | Challenging | Analytic | Budgeting and Responsibility | Budget Preparation | Application | 2.5 hours | X |
| Pr22-4B | 22-5 | Cash budget | Challenging | Analytic | Budgeting and Responsibility | Budget Preparation | Application | 2 hours | X |
| Pr22-5B | 22-4, 22-5 | Budgeted income statement and balance sheet | Challenging | Analytic | Budgeting and Responsibility | Budget Preparation | Application | 2 hours | X |
| CP22-1 | 22-1 | Ethics and professional conduct in business | Moderate | Ethics | Budgeting and Responsibility | Budget Preparation | Analysis | 20 min. | |
| CP22-2 | 22-1, 22-2 | Evaluating budgeting systems | Moderate | Analytic | Budgeting and Responsibility | Budget Preparation | Evaluation | 20 min. | |

| Problem | Learning Objective | Description | DIFFICULTY | BUSPROG Primary | ACBSP Primary | IMA Managerial Only | BLOOM'S | TIME | Spread-sheet |
|---------|---------|-------------|------------|----------------|---------------|---------------------|---------|------|--------------|
| CP22-3 | 22-2 | Service company static decision making | Moderate | Analytic | Budgeting and Responsibility | Budget Preparation | Application | 15 min. | |
| CP22-4 | 22-3 | Objectives of the master budget | Easy | Analytic | Budgeting and Responsibility | Budget Preparation | Analysis | 15 min. | |
| CP22-5 | 22-3 | Integrity and evaluating budgeting systems | Moderate | Analytic | Budgeting and Responsibility | Budget Preparation | Evaluation | 20 min. | |
| CP22-6 | 22-2 | Budget for a state government | Moderate | Analytic | Budgeting and Responsibility | Budget Preparation | Application | 1 hour | |

# Performance Evaluation Using Variances from Standard Costs

## OPENING COMMENTS

Standard cost systems set budgets for the materials, labor, and factory overhead used by a manufacturer to produce its product. Deviations from these standards are reported as variances.

After studying the chapter, your students should be able to:

1. Describe the types of standards and how they are established.

2. Describe and illustrate how standards are used in budgeting.

3. Compute and interpret direct materials and direct labor variances.

4. Compute and interpret factory overhead controllable and volume variances.

5. Journalize the entries for recording standards in the accounts and prepare an income statement that includes variances from standard.

6. Describe and provide examples of nonfinancial performance measures.

## STUDENT FAQS

- Do we need to know all these variance formulas? If so, is there a shortcut method we can use to calculate the six formulas?

- What is a standard, and why can it vary from company to company?

- How often should a standard change?

- Why does management need to evaluate variances and make adjustments?

- Factory overhead is divided into fixed and variable costs. Why not call volume, fixed and controllable, variable? It is easier to remember.

- Remind me again, what's the difference between "applied" and "budgeted"?

- What do volume and controllable variances *really* mean?

# OBJECTIVE 1

Describe the types of standards and how they are established.

## KEY TERMS

Currently Attainable Standards      Standard Cost Systems
Ideal Standards      Standards
Standard Cost

## SUGGESTED APPROACH

Manufacturing firms set standards for the amount and price of direct materials, direct labor, and overhead consumed by their products. Standards establish a benchmark to be used in evaluating actual performance. They allow management to recognize when costs are not in line with the company's projections and to take corrective action.

Ask your students to describe examples of standards in their daily lives. Examples include maximum and minimum speed limits on highways or rating scales on video games (such as novice, expert, etc.)

This objective also discusses the motivational impact of standards and when they should be revised. Stress the following points:

1. Unrealistically high standards frustrate employees and stifle motivation. As a result, most companies do not use *theoretical standards*, which can be achieved only under perfect operating conditions.
2. Standards that are too low encourage employees to be inefficient. Most companies use currently attainable standards (*normal standards*), which can be achieved with reasonable effort.
3. Standards should be changed when they no longer reflect operating conditions. They should not be revised simply because workers fail to meet standards.

## CLASS DISCUSSION — Motivational Impact of Standards

Ask your students to discuss whether they view the grading standards of this course, or other college courses, as ideal (theoretical standards) or normal (currently attainable standards). Ask them to comment on how grading standards impact their motivation to study and complete assignments.

# OBJECTIVE 2

**Describe and illustrate how standards are used in budgeting.**

## KEY TERMS

Budget Performance Report                 Total Manufacturing Cost Variance
Cost Variances                            Unfavorable Cost Variance
Favorable Cost Variance

## SUGGESTED APPROACH

Budgets exist to help companies plan, direct, and control operations. The budget performance report is a tool that compares actual costs to budgeted costs.

A sample budget performance report is presented in text Exhibit 2. Point out that the column labeled "Standard Cost at Actual Volume" is essentially a flexible budget. Flexible budgets were introduced in Chapter 22.

The following example can be used to illustrate performance measurement under standard costing. Assume a pizza company has set $5 as the standard cost of ingredients per pizza. The company anticipates selling 1,000 pizzas during the next week. The budget at the beginning of the week would be $5,000. This amount would be used for planning.

Now, assume the actual number of pizzas sold during the week was 1,200. The standard cost for ingredients to make 1,200 pizzas is $6,000. If the pizza parlor actually used $6,900 in ingredients during the week, there is a $900 variance from standard. This is an unfavorable variance since actual costs exceeded the standard cost for 1,200 pizzas.

This information would be presented on a budget performance report as follows:

|                   | Actual Cost | Standard Cost at Actual Volume (1,200 pizzas) | Cost Variance (Favorable)/Unfavorable |
|-------------------|-------------|-----------------------------------------------|----------------------------------------|
| Pizza Ingredients | $6,900      | $6,000                                        | $900                                   |

Management should investigate to determine whether this variance resulted from using ingredients that were more expensive than anticipated or from using more ingredients per pizza than budgeted. Note that comparing the $6,900 actual cost to the $5,000 original budget is not meaningful.

# OBJECTIVE 3

Compute and interpret direct materials and direct labor variances.

## KEY TERMS

Direct Labor Rate Variance                 Direct Materials Price Variance

Direct Labor Time Variance                 Direct Materials Quantity Variance

## SUGGESTED APPROACH — Direct Material

Variances are a perplexing topic for many students. As a result, you will probably need to dedicate significant class time to this topic. For materials variances, demonstrate how each variance is calculated and give your students the opportunity to practice these calculations using group learning activities.

## DEMONSTRATION PROBLEM — Direct Materials Variances

To demonstrate materials variances, use the following data for Martin Manufacturing during the month of November.

Standard: 5 pounds of direct materials are required per unit at $3.20 per pound

Actual: 104,000 pounds were used to produce 20,000 units; actual materials cost was $3.15 per pound

*Price Variance:* Emphasize that a direct materials price variance shows the difference between the actual and standard price for the actual quantity of materials used. The formula for this calculation is:

(Actual Price per Unit – Standard Price per Unit) × Actual Quantity Used
(AP – SP) × AQ Used

Using the data from Martin Manufacturing:

($3.15 – $3.20) × 104,000 = $5,200 favorable price variance

This variance is favorable because the materials cost $0.05 less per pound than standard.

*Quantity Variance:* Emphasize that the direct materials quantity variance shows the difference between the actual and standard quantity of materials used. This difference is measured at the standard price because the effect of the $0.05 per pound price savings was computed in the price variance. The formula to compute the quantity variance is:

(Actual Quantity Used – Standard Quantity) × Standard Price per Unit
(AQ Used – SQ) × SP per Unit

Using the data from Martin Manufacturing:

$(104,000 - 100,000) \times \$3.20 = \$12,800$ unfavorable quantity variance

Note that the standard quantity is 100,000 (5 lbs. per unit × 20,000 units actually produced). This variance is unfavorable because Martin used 4,000 more pounds than standard.

*Total Variance:* The total materials variance is the difference between the actual and standard cost of materials. It may be computed as follows:

(Actual Quantity × Actual Price per Unit) – (Standard Quantity × Standard Price per Unit)
(AQ × AP per Unit) – (SQ × SP per Unit)

Using the data from Martin Manufacturing:

$(104,000$ pounds $\times \$3.15$ per pound$) - (100,000$ pounds $\times \$3.20$ per pound$)$
    $= \$327,600 - \$320,000$
    $= \$7,600$ unfavorable total direct materials cost variance

The total variance may also be computed as follows:

| | |
|---|---|
| Price variance | $ 5,200 favorable |
| Quantity variance | 12,800 unfavorable |
| Total variance | $ 7,600 unfavorable |

## GROUP LEARNING ACTIVITY — Direct Materials Variances

Transparency Master (TM) 23-1 presents standard and actual cost data for direct materials used by Brass Works, Inc., a manufacturer of brass lamps and gift products. Instruct your students to compute materials price and quantity variances for Brass Works, Inc. The solution to this activity is on TM 23-2.

## CLASS DISCUSSION — Interpreting Materials Variances

As you review the solution to the group learning activity above (TM 23-2), ask your students to identify which department of Brass Works, Inc. should be held accountable for each variance. Also ask them to brainstorm possible reasons for the variance. Some examples follow:

| | Amount | Responsibility | Possible Reason(s) for Variance |
|---|---|---|---|
| Materials Price Variance | $420 U | Purchasing Department | Price increase from supplier. Extra freight charge on a rush order. |
| Materials Quantity Variance | $250 U | Production Department | Waste due to machine malfunction. Poor quality materials. |

## SUGGESTED APPROACH — Direct Labor

The labor rate and time variances closely mirror the materials price and quantity variances. As you present the formulas to calculate labor variances, stress the similarity to the materials variances. Ask your students to apply these formulas using a Group Learning Activity.

## LECTURE AID — Direct Labor Variances

Differences between actual and standard labor costs are analyzed by computing a rate and a time variance. The labor rate variance essentially performs the same analysis as the materials price variance. It computes the cost difference due to a change in labor rate. The formula for the rate variance is:

(Actual Rate per Hour – Standard Rate per Hour) × Actual Hours Worked

(AR per Hour – SR per Hour) × AH Worked

The labor time variance computes the labor cost difference due to using more or less labor time than standard. This variance parallels the materials quantity variance. The formula is:

(Actual Hours Worked – Standard Hours) × Standard Rate per Hour

(AH Worked – SH) × SR per Hour

Ask your students to identify which labor variances could be caused by new employees. Answer: New employees will usually create an unfavorable time variance as they learn their job. They may also cause a favorable rate variance if standards were based on wages earned by experienced employees and the new employee wage rate is below that amount.

## GROUP LEARNING ACTIVITY — Direct Labor Variances

TM 23-3 presents labor data for Brass Works, Inc. Ask your students to work in groups to calculate labor rate and time variances using the above formulas. The solution is shown on TM 23-4.

## CLASS DISCUSSION — Interpreting Materials Variances

As you review the solution on TM 23-4, ask your students to identify which department of Brass Works, Inc. should be held accountable for each labor variance. Also ask them to brainstorm possible reasons for the variance. Some examples follow:

| | Amount | Responsibility | Possible Reason(s) for Variance |
|---|---|---|---|
| Labor Rate Variance | $2,380 F | Production Department | Workers at lower wage rate assigned to job (e.g., temporary employees, less-skilled workers). |
| Labor Time Variance | $3,800 U | Production Department | Extra labor time required due to poor quality materials. Extra labor time required due to machine malfunctions. |

## SUGGESTED APPROACH — Nonmanufacturing Businesses

Standards can be applied to nonmanufacturing businesses, provided that they use repetitive activities to produce a common product or service. For example, businesses that specialize in fast, no-appointment-needed oil changes provide a standard service comprised of repetitive activities. A standard cost to perform an oil change could be developed based on the (1) standard labor time to change a customer's oil, (2) standard wage rate, (3) standard quantity of supplies used (motor oil, filters, etc.), and (4) standard price of supplies.

Public accounting firms are another example of businesses that rely heavily upon standards. Budgets and standards are used to measure performance on various client engagements, such as audits and tax work.

## WRITING EXERCISE — Standards in a Nonmanufacturing Environment

Ask your students to answer the following in writing (TM 23-8).

> Describe a nonmanufacturing business that could benefit from the use of standards. Also explain how standards would help that business control its operations.

**Possible response**: One example of a business that could benefit from the use of standards in a nonmanufacturing environment would be medical or legal transcription. The number of words transcribed per minute is an easy measurement to determine how employees are performing against a standard. Labor rates are also easy to track in this environment. This is only one example; your students should provide additional examples to discuss.

# OBJECTIVE 4

**Compute and interpret factory overhead controllable and volume variances.**

## KEY TERMS

Budgeted Variable Factory Overhead                    Factory Overhead Cost Variance Report
Controllable Variance                                              Volume Variance

## SUGGESTED APPROACH

Consider spending extra time covering factory overhead variances, since students seem to have the most difficulty with these variances. One of the major reasons for this is that, while direct materials and direct labor costs are variable, factory overhead costs have both fixed and variable components. You can continue the pattern of demonstrating variance calculations and asking students to practice these computations, using the aids below.

# DEMONSTRATION PROBLEM — Overhead Variances

In most cases, factory overhead costs are applied to production, using a predetermined factory overhead rate, calculated as follows:

$$\frac{\text{Estimated Total Factory Overhead Costs}}{\text{Estimated Activity Base (or Driver)}} \quad \text{(e.g., direct labor or machine hours)}$$

Factory overhead variances result when factory overhead applied to products does not equal actual overhead. Therefore, factory overhead variances occur whenever:

1. Factory overhead costs were greater or less than estimated.
2. The company operated above or below the capacity anticipated when estimating the activity driver.

Use the following data to illustrate factory overhead variances.

Martin Manufacturing applies factory overhead to products using direct labor hours. To calculate a predetermined overhead rate, Martin developed the following estimates for one month of production.

| | |
|---|---|
| Direct labor hours at 100 percent of normal capacity | 12,000 hrs. |
| Estimated fixed factory overhead costs | $120,000 |
| Estimated variable factory overhead costs at 100 percent of normal capacity | $ 84,000 |

As a result, Martin's predetermined factory overhead rate is $17 per direct labor hour. Of that rate, fixed factory overhead is $10 per hour ($120,000/12,000 hrs.) and variable factory overhead is $7 per hour ($84,000/12,000 hrs.).

Martin's labor standards allow 0.5 direct labor hours for each unit produced. During November, 20,000 units were produced. Actual fixed factory overhead costs were $120,000. Actual variable factory overhead costs were $88,000.

*Variable Factory Overhead Controllable Variance:* The text defines this variance as the difference between actual variable overhead costs and variable overhead budgeted for the amount of product actually produced. (Note that the text is essentially presenting a two-way overhead analysis.) This can be expressed in the following formula:

Actual Var. OH − (Var. OH Rate per Hr. × Units Produced × Standard Hrs. per Unit)

Using data from Martin Manufacturing:

Actual Variable Factory Overhead = $88,000
Budgeted Variable Factory Overhead for
  Actual Amount Produced = $7 × 20,000 units × 0.50 hrs. per unit = $70,000

Controllable Variance = $88,000 − $70,000 = $18,000 unfavorable

*Fixed Factory Overhead Volume Variance:* This variance measures the difference between the budgeted fixed overhead at 100 percent of normal capacity and the standard fixed overhead for the amount of product actually produced. In essence, it measures the impact of spreading fixed overhead over the wrong number of units, whenever actual production does not equal the amount anticipated by the predetermined fixed overhead rate. This can be expressed in the following formula:

(Hrs. at 100% of normal capacity – Std. Hrs. for Actual Production) × Fixed OH Rate per Hr.

Remind students that the term "Hrs. at 100% of normal capacity" is the hours used in computing the predetermined overhead rate.

Using the data from Martin Manufacturing:

(12,000 hours – 10,000 hours) × $10 per hr. = $20,000 unfavorable

Therefore, Martin's total overhead variance is as follows:

| | |
|---|---|
| Controllable variance | $ 18,000 unfavorable |
| Volume variance | 20,000 unfavorable |
| Total overhead variance | $ 38,000 unfavorable |

Emphasize that the total factory overhead variance is also the difference between actual overhead costs and overhead applied using a predetermined overhead rate. Therefore, the $38,000 unfavorable total factory overhead variance also represents $38,000 of underapplied overhead. The concept of over- and underapplied overhead was introduced in Chapter 19 when covering Job Order Costing.

## GROUP LEARNING ACTIVITY — Overhead Variances

TM 23-5 presents data for your students to use in calculating overhead variances. The solution to the exercise is provided on TM 23-6.

# OBJECTIVE 5

**Journalize the entries for recording standards in the accounts and prepare an income statement that includes variances from standard.**

## SUGGESTED APPROACH

Some companies choose to integrate standards and variances into their accounting records. When this occurs, entries to the materials, work in process, and finished goods inventory accounts are recorded at standard, not actual, costs. It is helpful to illustrate these entries for your students. A demonstration problem is included below for that purpose.

## DEMONSTRATION PROBLEM — Journal Entries at Standard

The group learning activities under Objectives 3 and 4 asked your students to compute materials and labor variances. Use these calculations to illustrate the following journal entries.

*Purchase of Materials:* Brass Works used 1,050 pounds of direct materials that cost $5.40 per pound. The effect of paying $0.40 more per pound than standard was a $420 unfavorable price variance. The purchase of these materials would be recorded as follows:

| | | |
|---|---|---|
| Materials (1,050 pounds × $5.00) | 5,250 | |
| Direct Materials Price Variance | 420 | |
|     Accounts Payable (1,050 pounds × $5.40) | | 5,670 |

Note that the Materials account is debited for the standard cost of materials purchased.

*Requisition of Materials:* Brass Works used 1,050 pounds of direct materials for production when the standard materials quantity was only 1,000 pounds. The effect of using more materials than standard is recorded when the materials are transferred to Work in Process.

| | | |
|---|---|---|
| Work in Process (1,000 pounds × $5.00) | 5,000 | |
| Direct Materials Quantity Variance | 250 | |
|     Materials (1,050 pounds × $5.00) | | 5,250 |

Note that the work in process account is debited for the standard price and quantity of materials. The materials account is credited for the actual quantity of materials used but at the standard price. The actual quantity of materials used must be removed from the account in order to have an accurate record of the amount of materials still on hand.

*Payment of Direct Labor Costs:* Brass Works incurred 2,380 direct labor hours at a cost of $9 per hour. The standard was 2,000 hours at $10 per hour. The payroll entry to record direct labor wages is:

| | | |
|---|---|---|
| Work in Process (2,000 hours × $10) | 20,000 | |
| Direct Labor Time Variance | 3,800 | |
|     Direct Labor Rate Variance | | 2,380 |
|     Wages Payable | | 21,420 |

The work in process account is debited for the standard labor rate and standard labor time.

Remind students that variances are usually transferred to Cost of Goods Sold at the end of the year. Unfavorable variances (resulting from costs above standard) increase Cost of Goods Sold; favorable variances (resulting from costs below standard) decrease Cost of Goods Sold. If variances are material, they should be allocated to Work in Process, Finished Goods, and Cost of Goods Sold.

## LECTURE AID — Reporting Variances on the Income Statement

Variances are not usually reported on financial statements prepared for stockholders, creditors, or other parties outside company management. However, they may be included on income statements prepared for management use. Exhibit 9 in the text provides an example of an income statement that reports variances. The key to this exhibit is understanding how the variances affect gross profit. Use the chart on TM 23-7 to explain the impact of favorable and unfavorable variances on gross profit.

# OBJECTIVE 6

**Describe and provide examples of nonfinancial performance measures.**

## KEY TERMS

Nonfinancial Performance Measure      Process

## SUGGESTED APPROACH

Measurements encourage improving the actions that are being measured. This is true both in the business world and in the classroom. Use the writing exercise below to stimulate your students to think about the benefits and difficulties of nonfinancial performance measures.

## WRITING EXERCISE — Nonfinancial Performance Measures

Ask your students to write their opinion on the following questions (TM 23-9):

> Students' scores on exams may be equated to financial measures used to evaluate employee performance in a business. Should college professors limit their evaluation of students to these "financial" measures? Do you see any potential benefits or disadvantages of including other measures of student performance in assigning course grades?

**Possible response**: Professors use optional measures to evaluate students all the time. Attendance, extra credit, and the subjective nature of some assignments provide options for evaluation on course work other than exam scores. Benefits include motivating students to put in extra time and effort to grasp the subject. In academia as in business, financial measures are not always the final or only performance measure.

## CLASS DISCUSSION — Nonfinancial Performance Measures

Ask your students to share examples of any nonfinancial measures used by their employers to evaluate their work. Question your students on why these measures are used. In other words, what behavior is the employer trying to encourage with these nonfinancial measures?

# HOMEWORK CHART WITH LEARNING OUTCOMES TAGGING

| Problem | Learning Objective | Description | DIFFICULTY | BUSPROG Primary | ACBSP Primary | IMA Managerial Only | BLOOM'S | TIME | Spread-sheet | GL |
|---|---|---|---|---|---|---|---|---|---|---|
| DQ23-1 | 23-1 | | Easy | Analytic | Budgeting and Responsibility | Performance Measurement | Knowledge | 5 min. | | |
| DQ23-2 | 23-1 | | Easy | Analytic | Budgeting and Responsibility | Performance Measurement | Knowledge | 5 min. | | |
| DQ23-3 | 23-3 | | Easy | Analytic | Budgeting and Responsibility | Performance Measurement | Knowledge | 5 min. | | |
| DQ23-4 | 23-2 | | Easy | Analytic | Budgeting and Responsibility | Performance Measurement | Knowledge | 5 min. | | |
| DQ23-5 | 23-3 | | Easy | Analytic | Budgeting and Responsibility | Performance Measurement | Knowledge | 5 min. | | |
| DQ23-6 | 23-3 | | Easy | Analytic | Budgeting and Responsibility | Performance Measurement | Knowledge | 5 min. | | |
| DQ23-7 | 23-3 | | Easy | Analytic | Budgeting and Responsibility | Performance Measurement | Knowledge | 5 min. | | |
| DQ23-8 | 23-4 | | Easy | Analytic | Budgeting and Responsibility | Performance Measurement | Knowledge | 5 min. | | |
| DQ23-9 | 23-5 | | Easy | Analytic | Budgeting and Responsibility | Performance Measurement | Knowledge | 5 min. | | |
| DQ23-10 | 23-6 | | Easy | Analytic | Budgeting and Responsibility | Performance Measurement | Knowledge | 5 min. | | |
| PE23-1A | 23-3 | Direct materials variances | Easy | Analytic | Budgeting and Responsibility | Performance Measurement | Application | 10 min. | | |
| PE23-1B | 23-3 | Direct materials variances | Easy | Analytic | Budgeting and Responsibility | Performance Measurement | Application | 10 min. | | |
| PE23-2A | 23-3 | Direct labor variances | Easy | Analytic | Budgeting and Responsibility | Performance Measurement | Application | 10 min. | | |
| PE23-2B | 23-3 | Direct labor variances | Easy | Analytic | Budgeting and Responsibility | Performance Measurement | Application | 10 min. | | |
| PE23-3A | 23-4 | Factory overhead controllable variance | Easy | Analytic | Budgeting and Responsibility | Performance Measurement | Application | 5 min. | | |
| PE23-3B | 23-4 | Factory overhead controllable variance | Easy | Analytic | Budgeting and Responsibility | Performance Measurement | Application | 5 min. | | |
| PE23-4A | 23-4 | Factory overhead volume variance | Easy | Analytic | Budgeting and Responsibility | Performance Measurement | Application | 5 min. | | |
| PE23-4B | 23-4 | Factory overhead volume variance | Easy | Analytic | Budgeting and Responsibility | Performance Measurement | Application | 5 min. | | |
| PE23-5A | 23-5 | Standard cost journal entries | Easy | Analytic | Budgeting and Responsibility | Performance Measurement | Application | 5 min. | | |
| PE23-5B | 23-5 | Standard cost journal entries | Easy | Analytic | Budgeting and Responsibility | Performance Measurement | Application | 5 min. | | |

| Problem | Learning Objective | Description | DIFFICULTY | BUSPROG Primary | ACBSP Primary | IMA Managerial Only | BLOOM'S | TIME | Spread-sheet | GL |
|---|---|---|---|---|---|---|---|---|---|---|
| PE23-6A | 23-5 | Income statement with variances | Easy | Analytic | Budgeting and Responsibility | Performance Measurement | Application | 15 min. | | |
| PE23-6B | 23-5 | Income statement with variances | Easy | Analytic | Budgeting and Responsibility | Performance Measurement | Application | 15 min. | | |
| PE23-7A | 23-6 | Activity inputs and outputs | Easy | Analytic | Budgeting and Responsibility | Performance Measurement | Knowledge | 5 min. | | |
| PE23-7B | 23-6 | Activity inputs and outputs | Easy | Analytic | Budgeting and Responsibility | Performance Measurement | Knowledge | 5 min. | | |
| Ex23-1 | 23-2 | Standard direct materials cost per unit | Easy | Analytic | Budgeting and Responsibility | Performance Measurement | Application | 10 min. | | |
| Ex23-2 | 23-2 | Standard product cost | Easy | Analytic | Budgeting and Responsibility | Performance Measurement | Application | 10 min. | | |
| Ex23-3 | 23-2 | Budget performance report | Moderate | Analytic | Budgeting and Responsibility | Performance Measurement | Application | 20 min. | X | |
| Ex23-4 | 23-3 | Direct materials variances | Easy | Analytic | Budgeting and Responsibility | Performance Measurement | Application | 10 min. | | |
| Ex23-5 | 23-3 | Direct material variances | Easy | Analytic | Budgeting and Responsibility | Performance Measurement | Application | 10 min. | | |
| Ex23-6 | 23-2, 23-3 | Standard direct materials cost per unit from variance data | Moderate | Analytic | Budgeting and Responsibility | Performance Measurement | Application | 15 min. | | |
| Ex23-7 | 23-2, 23-3 | Standard product cost, direct materials variance | Moderate | Analytic | Budgeting and Responsibility | Performance Measurement | Application | 15 min. | | |
| Ex23-8 | 23-3 | Direct labor variances | Easy | Analytic | Budgeting and Responsibility | Performance Measurement | Application | 10 min. | | |
| Ex23-9 | 23-3, 23-5 | Direct labor variances | Moderate | Analytic | Budgeting and Responsibility | Performance Measurement | Application | 15 min. | | |
| Ex23-10 | 23-3 | Direct labor variances | Easy | Analytic | Budgeting and Responsibility | Performance Measurement | Application | 10 min. | | |
| Ex23-11 | 23-3 | Direct labor standards for nonmanufacturing expenses | Moderate | Analytic | Budgeting and Responsibility | Performance Measurement | Application | 15 min. | | |
| Ex23-12 | 23-2, 23-3 | nonmanufacturing operations | Easy | Analytic | Budgeting and Responsibility | Performance Measurement | Application | 15 min. | | |
| Ex23-13 | 23-3 | Direct materials and direct labor variances | Moderate | Analytic | Budgeting and Responsibility | Performance Measurement | Application | 15 min. | | |
| Ex23-14 | 23-4 | Flexible overhead budget | Moderate | Analytic | Budgeting and Responsibility | Performance Measurement | Application | 30 min. | | |
| Ex23-15 | 23-4 | Flexible overhead budget | Moderate | Analytic | Budgeting and Responsibility | Performance Measurement | Application | 30 min. | | |
| Ex23-16 | 23-4 | Factory overhead cost variances | Moderate | Analytic | Budgeting and Responsibility | Performance Measurement | Application | 20 min. | | |
| Ex23-17 | 23-4 | Factory overhead cost variances | Easy | Analytic | Budgeting and Responsibility | Performance Measurement | Application | 15 min. | X | |

| Problem | Learning Objective | Description | DIFFICULTY | BUSPROG Primary | ACBSP Primary | IMA Managerial Only | BLOOM'S | TIME | Spreadsheet | GL |
|---|---|---|---|---|---|---|---|---|---|---|
| Ex23-18 | 23-4 | Factory overhead variance corrections | Moderate | Analytic | Budgeting and Responsibility | Performance Measurement | Application | 20 min. | | |
| Ex23-19 | 23-4 | Factory overhead cost variance report | Moderate | Analytic | Budgeting and Responsibility | Performance Measurement | Application | 30 min. | X | |
| Ex23-20 | 23-5 | Recording standards in accounts | Easy | Analytic | Budgeting and Responsibility | Performance Measurement | Application | 10 min. | | |
| Ex23-21 | 23-5 | Recording standards in accounts | Easy | Analytic | Budgeting and Responsibility | Performance Measurement | Application | 10 min. | | |
| Ex23-22 | 23-5 | Income statement indicating standard cost variances | Moderate | Analytic | Budgeting and Responsibility | Performance Measurement | Application | 20 min. | | |
| Ex23-23 | 23-6 | Nonfinancial performance measures | Easy | Analytic | Budgeting and Responsibility | Performance Measurement | Knowledge | 10 min. | | |
| Ex23-24 | 23-6 | Nonfinancial performance measures | Easy | Analytic | Budgeting and Responsibility | Performance Measurement | Knowledge | 10 min. | | |
| Pr23-1A | 23-2, 23-3 | Direct materials and direct labor variance and analysis | Moderate | Analytic | Budgeting and Responsibility | Performance Measurement | Application | 1 hour | | |
| Pr23-2A | 23-1, 23-2, 23-3 | Flexible budgeting and variance analysis | Moderate | Analytic | Budgeting and Responsibility | Performance Measurement | Application | 1.5 hours | X | |
| Pr23-3A | 23-3, 23-4 | Direct materials, direct labor, and factory overhead cost variance analysis | Moderate | Analytic | Budgeting and Responsibility | Performance Measurement | Application | 1 hour | X | |
| Pr23-4A | 23-4 | Standard factory overhead variance report | Challenging | Analytic | Budgeting and Responsibility | Performance Measurement | Application | 1 hour | X | X |
| Pr23-5A | 23-3, 23-6 | Standards for nonmanufacturing expenses | Moderate | Analytic | Budgeting and Responsibility | Performance Measurement | Application | 1.5 hours | | |
| Pr23-1B | 23-2, 23-3 | Direct materials and direct labor variance and analysis | Moderate | Analytic | Budgeting and Responsibility | Performance Measurement | Application | 1 hour | | |
| Pr23-2B | 23-1, 23-2, 23-3 | Flexible budgeting and variance analysis | Moderate | Analytic | Budgeting and Responsibility | Performance Measurement | Application | 1.5 hours | X | |
| Pr23-3B | 23-3, 23-4 | Direct materials, direct labor, and factory overhead cost variance analysis | Moderate | Analytic | Budgeting and Responsibility | Performance Measurement | Application | 1 hour | | |
| Pr23-4B | 23-4 | Standard factory overhead variance report | Challenging | Analytic | Budgeting and Responsibility | Performance Measurement | Application | 1 hour | X | X |
| Pr23-5B | 23-3, 23-6 | Standards for nonmanufacturing expenses | Moderate | Analytic | Budgeting and Responsibility | Performance Measurement | Application | 1.5 hours | | |
| Comp Problem 5 | 23-2, 23-3, 23-4, 23-5 | Break-even analysis, budgeting, and variance analysis | Challenging | Analytic | Budgeting and Responsibility | Performance Measurement | Application | 3 hours | | |
| CP23-1 | 23-1 | Ethics and professional conduct in business using nonmanufacturing standards | Easy | Ethics | Budgeting and Responsibility | Performance Measurement | Analysis | 15 min. | | |

| Problem | Learning Objective | Description | DIFFICULTY | BUSPROG | ACBSP | IMA | BLOOM'S | TIME | Spread-sheet | GL |
|---------|--------|-------------|------------|---------|-------|-----|---------|------|--------------|-----|
| | | | | Primary | Primary | Managerial Only | | | | |
| CP23-2 | 23-6 | Nonfinancial performance measures | Easy | Analytic | Budgeting and Responsibility | Performance Measurement | Analysis | 15 min. | | |
| CP23-3 | 23-3 | Variance interpretation | Moderate | Analytic | Budgeting and Responsibility | Performance Measurement | Evaluation | 30 min. | | |
| CP23-4 | 23-4 | Variance interpretation | Moderate | Analytic | Budgeting and Responsibility | Performance Measurement | Evaluation | 20 min. | | |
| CP23-5 | 23-6 | Nonmanufacturing performance measures—government | Moderate | Analytic | Budgeting and Responsibility | Performance Measurement | Application | 1 hour | | |

# Performance Evaluation for Decentralized Operations

## OPENING COMMENTS

Chapter 24 applies responsibility accounting to cost, profit, and investment centers. The chapter demonstrates the responsibility accounting reports that are used to evaluate department or division performance. This provides an excellent opportunity to remind your students that managers are judged, at least in part, using accounting data.

The chapter opens with a discussion of decentralized operations. It also illustrates transfer pricing under the market price, negotiated price, and cost price approaches.

After studying the chapter, your students should be able to:

1. Describe the advantages and disadvantages of decentralized operations.

2. Prepare a responsibility accounting report for a cost center.

3. Prepare responsibility accounting reports for a profit center.

4. Compute and interpret the rate of return on investment, the residual income, and the balanced scorecard for an investment center.

5. Describe and illustrate how the market price, negotiated price, and cost price approaches to transfer pricing may be used by decentralized segments of a business.

# STUDENT FAQS

- Why is decentralized management used when the managers usually don't have the experience or training?

- What is the best type of responsibility accounting center and why?

- What are considered invested assets on the balance sheet?

- Does management actually use all these formulas to determine if a company is doing well or not?

- Besides comparing to years in the past for a company, where do you get industrial averages?

# OBJECTIVE 1

Describe the advantages and disadvantages of decentralized operations.

## KEY TERM

Responsibility Accounting

## SUGGESTED APPROACH

You can cover this objective by using Transparency Master (TM) 24-1, which lists the advantages and disadvantages of decentralized operations.

As an alternative, ask your students to describe the advantages and disadvantages of a management position in a decentralized firm. TM 24-2 provides a manager's job description. Read this description to your class and ask them to point out any positive or negative aspects of the job.

**Possible response:** The decentralized operation of the real estate company allows the local office to react to the local market and needs of the agents. Every market will be different and to apply blanket advertising and management policies to each office would not be an effective way to maximize the potential of the local market. Possible disadvantages could be technology and communications. Allowing each individual office to make its own separate technology decisions could result in incompatibility issues. Other disadvantages include the local office making decisions that are contradictory to the overall goals of the corporation.

## CLASS DISCUSSION — Centralization versus Decentralization

Ask your students to characterize businesses they have worked for as either centralized or decentralized. Ask them to explain how they made that determination.

## LECTURE AID — Responsibility Centers

Objective 1 introduces the three types of responsibility centers. These are listed and described on TM 24-3. Review this information with your students. Ask your students whether their parents view them as a cost, profit, or investment center.

TM 24-4 presents various divisions/departments that would be found in a typical department store. Give your students a couple of minutes to read through the list and determine whether they would organize each unit as an investment, profit, or cost center. Ask them to share their answers with the class.

**Possible response to TM 24-4:**

1. Each of the five stores in the chain – Profit center or Investment center (see below)
2. Accounting department – Cost center
3. Ladies clothing department – Profit center
4. Furniture department – Profit center
5. Credit and collection department – Cost center

As students share their answers, emphasize the level of authority given to the manager of each unit based on the type of responsibility center. For example, if your students determine that each store in the chain should be an investment center, each store manager must have authority to make decisions regarding costs, sales strategies, and fixed assets purchased by his or her store (within company guidelines). If stores are considered profit centers, the store manager may have authority to control costs and sales strategies, but he or she would not make decisions regarding the purchase or disposal of fixed assets.

# OBJECTIVE 2

**Prepare a responsibility accounting report for a cost center.**

## KEY TERM

Cost Center

## SUGGESTED APPROACH

Managers of cost centers are evaluated by comparing actual costs against budgeted or standard costs. A responsibility report shows a cost center's actual and budgeted costs, as well as the amount by which the center is over or under budget.

You may use the reports illustrated in Exhibit 3 in the text to review responsibility accounting reports. As an alternative, ask students to generate a responsibility accounting report using the following Group Learning Activity.

## GROUP LEARNING ACTIVITY — Responsibility Accounting

TM 24-5 provides the organization chart for the accounting function of a corporation. Use this chart to illustrate that cost centers may exist within cost centers.

TM 24-6 shows budget performance reports for the accounting departments that report to the controller. Divide your class into small groups and instruct each group to prepare the responsibility accounting report that would be given to the corporate controller. A solution is displayed on TM 24-7.

This exercise will allow you to emphasize that upper-level managers receive summarized cost data. When reviewing TM 24-7, ask your students which departments the controller should question regarding their performance. You could also ask one or more students to assume the position of a department manager and explain his or her department's performance to the corporate controller.

# OBJECTIVE 3

Prepare responsibility accounting reports for a profit center.

## KEY TERMS

Controllable Expenses      Profit Center
Controllable Revenues      Service Department Charges

## SUGGESTED APPROACH

Under responsibility accounting, profit centers should be evaluated based only on revenues and expenses that can be controlled by the manager. Controllable expenses include expenses incurred directly by the department or the division, as well as service department charges. A charge allocated to a profit center from a service department (such as Personnel or Maintenance) is an example of an indirect expense. That charge is controllable if the profit center manager is free to choose how much of the service is used.

Use the Group Learning Activity below to cover the preparation of divisional income statements for profit centers.

## GROUP LEARNING ACTIVITY — Evaluating Profit Centers

Handout 24-1 presents information for Watson Clothiers, a business that operates stores in two cities. Ask your students to use the information to prepare divisional income statements using the concept of responsibility accounting. Under responsibility accounting, only controllable revenues and expenses are listed. You may want to refer your students to the sample statement presented in Exhibit 5 in the text. The solution is presented on TM 24-8.

Handout 24-1 includes a service department expense that is not controllable by Watson's store managers. Under the concept of responsibility accounting, this expense should not appear on divisional income statements. Any cost incurred that is not under the store manager's authority should not be used to evaluate their performance. In theory, these costs should appear only on a consolidated income statement for the entire company.

You may want to point out that, unfortunately, many organizations allocate uncontrollable charges to departments or divisions. This often leads to frustration for managers who must explain costs that are beyond their control.

## CLASS DISCUSSION — Controllable and Noncontrollable Indirect Costs

The following is a list of miscellaneous questions regarding the charging of indirect costs. Use these to spark discussion.

1. Why would an organization charge indirect service costs to the departments that use these services? (Answer: To bring a market discipline to the operating departments. If users are charged a fee for services, they will use services judiciously. In addition, if the operating department can choose to purchase services from the outside, internal service departments are motivated to remain efficient.)

2. Should any university administrative overhead be charged to academic departments or other responsibility centers? (Answer: yes. There are many university services that could be directly identified and charged to departments, such as copying, photographic services, computer support, and repairs and maintenance.)

3. What would be an appropriate activity base for charging central telephone services to departments within an organization? (Answer: number of phone lines)

4. Give an example of a noncontrollable cost for a manager of a McDonald's franchise. (Answer: Corporate advertising would not be controllable.)

# OBJECTIVE 4

Compute and interpret the rate of return on investment, the residual income, and the balanced scorecard for an investment center.

## KEY TERMS

Balanced Scorecard  
DuPont Formula  
Investment Center  
Investment Turnover  

Profit Margin  
Rate of Return on Investment (ROI)  
Residual Income

## SUGGESTED APPROACH

Remind students that investment centers are evaluated as if they were separate companies. Both profitability and efficiency in the use of assets must be judged. Most companies prepare a report that shows income from operations by investment center to evaluate profitability. Rate of return on investment or residual income is used to gauge asset efficiency.

Responsibility reports that show controllable revenues and controllable expenses by investment center are prepared using the same techniques covered in Objective 3. Use the following Demonstration Problem to illustrate rate of return on investment and residual income measures. After demonstrating these measures, use TM 24-9 to discuss the advantages and disadvantages of using rate of return on investment and residual income for performance evaluation.

## DEMONSTRATION PROBLEM — Return on Investment

The formula for rate of return on investment (ROI) is as follows:

$$ROI = \frac{\text{Income from Operations}}{\text{Invested Assets}}$$

Assume two divisions of a manufacturing company had the following sales, income from operations, and invested assets.

|  | Sales | Income from Operations | Invested Assets |
|---|---|---|---|
| Division A | $500,000 | $ 90,000 | $400,000 |
| Division B | 800,000 | 144,000 | 600,000 |

Give your students a minute to calculate the rate of return on assets for each division and write the answer in their notes. (Answer: Division A = 22.5 percent, Division B = 24.0 percent)

From this calculation, it appears that Division B is providing a greater return on the company's investment than Division A. This greater return could occur for one of two reasons: (1) Division B is more profitable or (2) Division B is using its assets more efficiently. To determine the underlying reason for Division B's performance, the rate of return on investment equation can be expanded using the *DuPont formula* as follows:

$$ROI = \frac{\text{Income from Operations}}{\text{Sales}} \times \frac{\text{Sales}}{\text{Invested Assets}}$$

or

$$ROI = \text{Profit Margin} \times \text{Investment Turnover}$$

Profit margin measures profitability by showing the percentage of profit earned on each sales dollar. Investment turnover measures asset usage by comparing assets to the amount of sales generated.

Ask your students to use the DuPont formula to calculate profit margin and investment turnover for both divisions. This analysis should yield the following information:

|  | Profit Margin | Investment Turnover | Rate of Return on Investment |
|---|---|---|---|
| Division A | 18% | 1.25 | 22.5% |
| Division B | 18% | 1.33 | 24.0% |

Stress that Divisions A and B have managed costs of goods sold and operating expenses to achieve an 18 percent profit. However, Division B has made more sales relative to its assets than Division A. Division B is using its assets more efficiently, bringing in more return on the company's investment.

## DEMONSTRATION PROBLEM — Residual Income

Residual income is the amount by which income from operations exceeds the minimum income considered accepta le by top management. The minimum acceptable income is normally determined by multiplying a minimu rate of return by the division's invested assets. The following equations may help your students remembe hese relationships:

Residual Income = In ome from Operations – Minimum Acceptable Income

Minimum Acceptable Inco e = Invested Assets × Minimum Rate of Return

Ask your students to calculate the resic al income for Divisions A and B, assuming that the company's minimum rate of return is 15 percent.

|  | Controllable Operating Income | | Minimum Acceptable Income | | Residual Income |
|---|---|---|---|---|---|
| Division A | $ 90,000 | – | $60,000 | = | $30,000 |
| Division B | $144,000 | – | $90,000 | = | $54,000 |

Point out that many firms use the term "Economic Value Added (EVA)" when referring to residual income.

## INTERNET ACTIVITY — Balanced Scorecard

The balanced scorecard emphasizes that financial and nonfinancial measures are both important in measuring the performance of an organization. In fact, the nonfinancial measures frequently focus management on items leading to the long-term success of an organization. The four components of the balanced scorecard are described in text Exhibit 7. These components are (1) Innovation and Learning, (2) Customer Service, (3) Internal Processes, and (4) Financial Performance.

Choose an organization (such as your college or university) and ask students to develop at least one measure in each of the four components of the balanced scorecard. For example, a measure in the innovation and learning category might be the number of classrooms converted for multimedia presentations.

Ask your students to perform an Internet search using "Balanced Scorecard" as the search criteria and ask them to report what types of items their search uncovers. Your students will find numerous links to consulting firms and companies that have developed software applications to assist with implementing a balanced scorecard. Some of these sites offer interesting insights on the balanced scorecard, but many are simply trying to sell their services. You can use this search to discuss the role of consultants in helping businesses apply new management ideas.

# OBJECTIVE 5

**Describe and illustrate how the market price, negotiated price, and cost price approaches to transfer pricing may be used by decentralized segments of a business.**

## KEY TERMS

Cost Price Approach            Negotiated Price Approach

Market Price Approach          Transfer Price

## SUGGESTED APPROACH

Use the Lecture Aids that follow to introduce students to the subject of transfer pricing. A simple role-playing activity can be effective in presenting the market price and negotiated price approach to transfer pricing.

## LECTURE AID — Transfer Pricing

In some cases, one division of a company may make products that are used by another division of that same company. For example, General Motors has separate divisions that make automobile components (such as engines, transmissions, and stereos). These divisions "sell" their component parts to divisions that assemble automobiles. The transfer price is the selling price credited to one division when its goods are transferred to another division.

TM 24-10 lists the benefits that are gained when transfer pricing is used in intercompany transfers. The information below will help you review that TM with your students.

**Benefits of Transfer Pricing**

1. Divisions can be evaluated as profit or investment centers.

   To be a profit or investment center, a division must have the ability to earn revenue. Transfer pricing allows a division to recognize revenue on intercompany sales. (NOTE: This revenue is recorded only for managerial accounting purposes. Companies cannot show revenue on sales to itself when preparing financial statements under financial accounting principles.)

2. Divisions are forced to control costs and operate competitively.

   For a division to show a profit, the transfer price received must exceed the cost to make a product.

3. If divisions are permitted to buy component parts wherever they can find the best price (either internally or externally), transfer pricing will allow a company to maximize its profits.

   If a component part can be produced cheaper by an outside company than an internal division, that part will be purchased from the outside. This forces the internal division to cut costs to the point that it competes with outside firms or is discontinued. In addition, the division manufacturing the component parts is free to sell to outside organizations whenever (1) there is excess capacity or (2) the outside organizations are willing to pay more than internal divisions.

Emphasize that transfer pricing can be used to turn any cost center into a profit center. For example, a company may have a printing department that duplicates company documents. That department could use a transfer price to charge other departments for its services. The same benefits of transfer pricing discussed in TM 24-10 apply to the printing department. It must keep its operating costs in line with outside printing firms, or departments that need printing and duplication services will take their business elsewhere.

## ROLE PLAYING — Market and Negotiated Transfer Prices

To illustrate market and negotiated transfer prices, choose two students to participate in a role-playing activity.

Explain to your students that they are managers of two divisions of a company that manufactures power tools. One manages the division that produces the small engines that drive the tools. The other manages the division that assembles the tools. Although the assembly division needs engines, it is free to purchase them from the engine division or an outside company, wherever the best price can be obtained.

In private, tell the engine division manager that his or her engines require $35 of variable costs to produce. They can be sold to outside companies for $50 per engine. Also tell the manager that his or her division is operating at full capacity and can sell all the engines it makes to outside firms at $50 each if the assembly division does not buy any of the engines.

Next, privately tell the assembly division manager that he or she needs to purchase 10,000 engines. Engines can be purchased from outside firms for $50 each. These engines are the same quality as those produced by the company's engine division.

Begin the role playing by asking the assembly division manager to "telephone" the engine division manager and negotiate a price for the engines. Because the engine division manager wants at least $50 per engine, and the assembly division manager will not pay more than $50, the two should settle on the market price of $50 for the transfer. After the trade is negotiated, share with the class the facts given to each manager. This will allow you to emphasize that a company can set transfer prices at market prices if divisions are operating at full capacity and can sell all their products.

Next, privately tell the engine division manager to assume that his or her division is not producing at full capacity. Therefore, he or she needs the assembly division's business. Remind the student that his or her division's profits will be increased as long as the engines are sold for more than their variable cost of $35.

Next, in private, tell the assembly division manager to assume the same information as before: He or she needs 10,000 engines, which can be purchased for $50 from an outside organization.

Allow the students to negotiate for a few minutes. The agreed-on transfer price will be based, in part, on who is the best negotiator. In any case, however, it should be between $35 and $50. At the end of the role play, ask the engine division manager to explain why he or she was willing to accept less than $50 for the engines. This will allow you to show that transfer prices can be negotiated if excess capacity exists. Emphasize that negotiated transfer prices will fall in the range between variable cost and market price in order for both the buyer and seller to benefit.

## LECTURE AID — Transfer Pricing at Cost

Remind students that some companies transfer products at their cost. This cost may be the division's variable cost per unit or the total cost per unit. In addition, the products may be transferred at actual or standard cost.

Most companies tend to transfer products at standard cost. If actual cost is used, divisions are permitted to pass any unfavorable variances on to the divisions buying their products. As a result, supplying divisions are not motivated to control costs when transfer prices are based on actual costs.

# PERFORMANCE REPORT FOR PROFIT CENTERS

Watson Clothiers, a retailer specializing in men's and ladies' career clothing, has stores in two Ohio cities: Cincinnati and Columbus. These stores are evaluated as profit centers.

Sales and direct costs for the stores in the current year were as follows:

|  | Cincinnati | Columbus |
|---|---|---|
| Net sales | $220,000 | $380,000 |
| Cost of goods sold | 80,000 | 152,000 |
| Sales salaries | 32,000 | 45,000 |
| Property taxes, utilities, and depreciation | 16,000 | 19,000 |
| Miscellaneous operating expenses | 1,000 | 2,000 |

The following indirect costs were incurred by service departments at Watson Clothiers in the current year:

| General Administration | $83,000 |
|---|---|
| Personnel and Payroll | 49,000 |
| Advertising | 67,000 |

Store managers can control the services used from the Personnel and Payroll and the Advertising departments based on hiring and marketing decisions. They cannot control services provided by General Administration. Use of service department resources in the current year was as follows:

|  | Percent used by Cincinnati | Percent used by Columbus |
|---|---|---|
| Personnel and Payroll | 40% | 60% |
| Advertising | 25% | 75% |

Required: Prepare divisional income statements for Watson Clothiers, showing each store's income from operations. In accordance with responsibility accounting, include only controllable revenues and controllable expenses.

# HOMEWORK CHART WITH LEARNING OUTCOMES TAGGING

| Problem | Learning Objective | Description | DIFFICULTY | BUSPROG Primary | ACBSP Primary | IMA Managerial Only | BLOOM'S | TIME | Spread-sheet |
|---|---|---|---|---|---|---|---|---|---|
| DQ24-1 | 24-2 | | Easy | Analytic | Budgeting and Responsibility | Performance Measurement | Knowledge | 5 min. | |
| DQ24-2 | 24-2 | | Easy | Analytic | Budgeting and Responsibility | Performance Measurement | Knowledge | 5 min. | |
| DQ24-3 | 24-3 | | Easy | Analytic | Budgeting and Responsibility | Performance Measurement | Knowledge | 5 min. | |
| DQ24-4 | 24-4 | | Easy | Analytic | Budgeting and Responsibility | Performance Measurement | Knowledge | 5 min. | |
| DQ24-5 | 24-4 | | Easy | Analytic | Budgeting and Responsibility | Performance Measurement | Knowledge | 5 min. | |
| DQ24-6 | 24-4 | | Easy | Analytic | Budgeting and Responsibility | Performance Measurement | Knowledge | 5 min. | |
| DQ24-7 | 24-4 | | Easy | Analytic | Budgeting and Responsibility | Performance Measurement | Knowledge | 5 min. | |
| DQ24-8 | 24-5 | | Easy | Analytic | Budgeting and Responsibility | Performance Measurement | Knowledge | 5 min. | |
| DQ24-9 | 24-5 | | Easy | Analytic | Budgeting and Responsibility | Performance Measurement | Knowledge | 5 min. | |
| DQ24-10 | 24-5 | | Easy | Analytic | Budgeting and Responsibility | Performance Measurement | Knowledge | 5 min. | |
| PE24-1A | 24-2 | Budgetary performance for cost center | Easy | Analytic | Budgeting and Responsibility | Performance Measurement | Application | 5 min. | |
| PE24-1B | 24-2 | Budgetary performance for cost center | Easy | Analytic | Budgeting and Responsibility | Performance Measurement | Application | 5 min. | |
| PE24-2A | 24-3 | Service department charges | Easy | Analytic | Budgeting and Responsibility | Performance Measurement | Application | 5 min. | |
| PE24-2B | 24-3 | Service department charges | Easy | Analytic | Budgeting and Responsibility | Performance Measurement | Application | 5 min. | |
| PE24-3A | 24-3 | Income from operations for profit center | Easy | Analytic | Budgeting and Responsibility | Performance Measurement | Application | 5 min. | |
| PE24-3B | 24-3 | Income from operations for profit center | Easy | Analytic | Budgeting and Responsibility | Performance Measurement | Application | 5 min. | |
| PE24-4A | 24-4 | Profit margin, investment turnover, and ROI | Easy | Analytic | Budgeting and Responsibility | Performance Measurement | Application | 10 min. | |
| PE24-4B | 24-4 | Profit margin, investment turnover, and ROI | Easy | Analytic | Budgeting and Responsibility | Performance Measurement | Application | 10 min. | |
| PE24-5A | 24-4 | Residual income | Easy | Analytic | Budgeting and Responsibility | Performance Measurement | Application | 5 min. | |
| PE24-5B | 24-4 | Residual income | Easy | Analytic | Budgeting and Responsibility | Performance Measurement | Application | 5 min. | |
| PE24-6A | 24-5 | Transfer pricing | Easy | Analytic | Budgeting and Responsibility | Performance Measurement | Application | 10 min. | |
| PE24-6B | 24-5 | Transfer pricing | Easy | Analytic | Budgeting and Responsibility | Performance Measurement | Application | 10 min. | |
| Ex24-1 | 24-2 | Budget performance reports for cost centers | Moderate | Analytic | Budgeting and Responsibility | Performance Measurement | Application | 15 min. | |
| Ex24-2 | 24-3 | Divisional income statements | Easy | Analytic | Budgeting and Responsibility | Performance Measurement | Application | 15 min. | |
| Ex24-3 | 24-3 | Service department charges and activity bases | Easy | Analytic | Budgeting and Responsibility | Performance Measurement | Application | 5 min. | |
| Ex24-4 | 24-3 | Activity bases for service department charges | Moderate | Analytic | Budgeting and Responsibility | Performance Measurement | Application | 15 min. | |
| Ex24-5 | 24-3 | Service department charges | Moderate | Analytic | Budgeting and Responsibility | Performance Measurement | Application | 20 min. | |
| Ex24-6 | 24-3 | Service department charges and activity bases | Moderate | Analytic | Budgeting and Responsibility | Performance Measurement | Application | 30 min. | |

| Problem | Learning Objective | Description | DIFFICULTY | BUSPROG Primary | ACBSP Primary | IMA Managerial Only | BLOOM'S | TIME | Spread-sheet |
|---------|-------------------|-------------|------------|-----------------|---------------|---------------------|---------|------|-------------|
| Ex24-7 | 24-3 | Divisional income statements with service department charges | Moderate | Analytic | Budgeting and Responsibility | Performance Measurement | Application | 20 min. | X |
| Ex24-8 | 24-3 | Corrections to service department charges | Moderate | Analytic | Budgeting and Responsibility | Performance Measurement | Application | 30 min. | |
| Ex24-9 | 24-3 | Profit center responsibility reporting | Moderate | Analytic | Budgeting and Responsibility | Performance Measurement | Application | 30 min. | X |
| Ex24-10 | 24-4 | Rate of return on investment | Easy | Analytic | Budgeting and Responsibility | Performance Measurement | Application | 15 min. | |
| Ex24-11 | 24-4 | Residual income | Easy | Analytic | Budgeting and Responsibility | Performance Measurement | Application | 15 min. | |
| Ex24-12 | 24-4 | Determining missing items in rate of return computation | Easy | Analytic | Budgeting and Responsibility | Performance Measurement | Application | 10 min. | |
| Ex24-13 | 24-4 | Profit margin, investment turnover, and rate of return on investment | Moderate | Analytic | Budgeting and Responsibility | Performance Measurement | Application | 20 min. | |
| Ex24-14 | 24-4 | Rate of return on investment | Moderate | Analytic | Budgeting and Responsibility | Performance Measurement | Application | 15 min. | |
| Ex24-15 | 24-4 | Determining missing items in rate of return and residual income computations | Moderate | Analytic | Budgeting and Responsibility | Performance Measurement | Application | 15 min. | |
| Ex24-16 | 24-4 | Determining missing items from computations | Moderate | Analytic | Budgeting and Responsibility | Performance Measurement | Application | 20 min. | |
| Ex24-17 | 24-4 | Rate of return on investment, residual income | Moderate | Analytic | Budgeting and Responsibility | Performance Measurement | Application | 15 min. | |
| Ex24-18 | 24-4 | Balanced scoreboard | Easy | Analytic | Budgeting and Responsibility | Performance Measurement | Application | 10 min. | |
| Ex24-19 | 24-4 | Balanced scoreboard | Moderate | Analytic | Budgeting and Responsibility | Performance Measurement | Application | 15 min. | |
| Ex24-20 | 24-5 | Decision on transfer pricing | Easy | Analytic | Budgeting and Responsibility | Performance Measurement | Application | 15 min. | |
| Ex24-21 | 24-5 | Decision on transfer pricing | Easy | Analytic | Budgeting and Responsibility | Performance Measurement | Application | 25 min. | |
| Pr24-1A | 24-2 | Budget performance report for a cost center | Moderate | Analytic | Budgeting and Responsibility | Performance Measurement | Application | 1 hour | X |
| Pr24-2A | 24-3 | Profit center responsibility reporting | Moderate | Analytic | Budgeting and Responsibility | Performance Measurement | Application | 1 hour | X |
| Pr24-3A | 24-4 | Divisional income statements and rate of return on investment analysis | Moderate | Analytic | Budgeting and Responsibility | Performance Measurement | Application | 45 min. | X |
| Pr24-4A | 24-4 | Effect of proposals on divisional performance | Moderate | Analytic | Budgeting and Responsibility | Performance Measurement | Application | 1.5 hours | X |
| Pr24-5A | 24-4 | Divisional performance analysis and evaluation | Moderate | Analytic | Budgeting and Responsibility | Performance Measurement | Application | 1 hour | X |
| Pr24-6A | 24-5 | Transfer pricing | Moderate | Analytic | Budgeting and Responsibility | Performance Measurement | Application | 1.5 hours | X |
| Pr24-1B | 24-2 | Budget performance report for a cost center | Moderate | Analytic | Budgeting and Responsibility | Performance Measurement | Application | 1 hour | X |
| Pr24-2B | 24-3 | Profit center responsibility reporting | Moderate | Analytic | Budgeting and Responsibility | Performance Measurement | Application | 1 hour | X |

| Problem | Learning Objective | Description | DIFFICULTY | BUSPROG Primary | ACBSP Primary | IMA Managerial Only | BLOOM'S | TIME | Spread-sheet |
|---|---|---|---|---|---|---|---|---|---|
| Pr24-3B | 24-4 | Divisional income statements and rate of return on investment analysis | Moderate | Analytic | Budgeting and Responsibility | Performance Measurement | Application | 45 min. | X |
| Pr24-4B | 24-4 | Effect of proposals on divisional performance | Moderate | Analytic | Budgeting and Responsibility | Performance Measurement | Application | 1.5 hours | X |
| Pr24-5B | 24-4 | Divisional performance analysis and evaluation | Moderate | Analytic | Budgeting and Responsibility | Performance Measurement | Application | 1 hour | X |
| Pr24-6B | 24-5 | Transfer pricing | Moderate | Analytic | Budgeting and Responsibility | Performance Measurement | Application | 1.5 hours | X |
| CP24-1 | 24-5 | Ethics and professional conduct in business | Easy | Ethics | Budgeting and Responsibility | Performance Measurement | Analysis | 20 min. | |
| CP24-2 | 24-3 | Service department charges | Easy | Analytic | Budgeting and Responsibility | Performance Measurement | Analysis | 15 min. | |
| CP24-3 | 24-4 | Evaluating divisional performance | Moderate | Analytic | Budgeting and Responsibility | Performance Measurement | Evaluation | 30 min. | |
| CP24-4 | 24-4 | Evaluating division performance over time | Moderate | Analytic | Budgeting and Responsibility | Performance Measurement | Evaluation | 30 min. | |
| CP24-5 | 24-4 | Evaluating division performance | Moderate | Analytic | Budgeting and Responsibility | Performance Measurement | Evaluation | 45 min. | |

# Differential Analysis, Product Pricing, and Activity-Based Costing

## OPENING COMMENTS

This chapter covers (1) differential analysis, (2) methods of determining the selling price of a product using a cost-plus markup approach, (3) the effects of production bottlenecks, and (4) activity-based costing. The cost-plus approach of product cost is described in Objective 2; total cost and variable cost methods are presented in the chapter appendix. All topics in this chapter are able to stand alone. Therefore, the instructor is free to cover only one or two of the topics if class time is a limited resource as the term draws to a close.

After studying the chapter, your students should be able to:

1. Prepare differential analysis reports for a variety of managerial decisions.

2. Determine the selling price of a product, using the product cost concept.

3. Compute the relative profitability of products in bottleneck production processes.

4. Allocate product costs using activity-based costing.

## STUDENT FAQS

- What are some guidelines I can use to decide which method to use to set a normal price for a product?

- How do you determine what your profit is in real life?

...ity-based costing (ABC) is better at identifying all the costs, why is it not used to
...mine inventory valuation or preparation of financial statements?

Why are proper cost driver uses so important in determining correct cost per item?

- Why is sunk cost never an item to consider in differential analysis?

# OBJECTIVE 1

Prepare differential analysis reports for a variety of managerial decisions.

## KEY TERMS

| | |
|---|---|
| Differential Analysis | Differential Revenue |
| Differential Cost | Opportunity Cost |
| Differential Income (Loss) | Sunk Cost |

## SUGGESTED APPROACH

Differential analysis is a method used to quantitatively evaluate alternative courses of action. Under differential analysis, the difference between the revenues and costs of alternatives is compared. The goal is to choose the alternative that results in the greatest amount of profit or the lowest cost.

Begin your discussion of differential analysis by using the Group Learning Activity that follows. This activity will ask your students to compare the differential revenues and expenses of two summer jobs.

Use the second Group Learning Activity to illustrate additional applications of differential analysis. Emphasize that your students should concentrate on understanding the broad concept of differential analysis rather than memorizing specific examples of how it is applied.

Wrap-up this objective by asking your students to give examples of decisions that should be evaluated using differential cost techniques. Also encourage them to consider the qualitative factors influencing business decisions through a Writing Exercise.

## GROUP LEARNING ACTIVITY — Introduction to Differential Analysis

Transparency Master (TM) 25-1 presents information concerning two summer jobs: one in an office and one at an amusement park. Divide your class into small groups and ask them to determine which job they would choose. Have each group record their choice and the supporting analysis.

Ask a few groups to present their answers in front of the class. Although the groups will probably reach the same conclusion, there may be significant variation in how they obtained this answer. Show TM 25-2, which presents a differential analysis report in the format used by the text. Under differential analysis, this problem is solved by comparing differential revenues to differential costs.

After reviewing the quantitative analysis, remind students that qualitative factors must be considered as well. Ask students to name qualitative factors that might influence them to take the amusement park job even though it pays less.

## GROUP LEARNING ACTIVITY — Differential Analysis

Handout 25-1 presents four differential analysis problems similar to those presented in the text. Divide the class into small groups to work on these problems.

Rather than asking each group to do all four problems, you may want to assign only one problem to each group. After giving the groups enough time to solve their problems, ask them to present their solutions to the class. This will give your students the opportunity to teach an example to the class.

As an alternative, ask the members of each small group to "count off" using the numbers one through four. Ask all the ones to gather in one corner of the room, all the twos in another corner, and so on. Assign each of these four large groups a problem to solve. After the groups are finished solving their problems, break up the large groups and ask the class to reassemble in their original small groups. Group member number one is then responsible for teaching the solution to problem one to his or her group. Continue this until all solutions have been taught. In this exercise, each group member becomes an expert on one type of differential analysis and shares his or her expertise with the group.

A solution to Handout 25-1 is provided in TMs 25-3 through 25-7.

## CLASS DISCUSSION — Differential Analysis

Ask your students to identify decisions from their personal experiences that fit under each of the categories of differential analysis presented in the text. For example, a decision to cook dinner or order a pizza is essentially a "make or buy" decision. Deciding whether to go to work or go on to graduate school after finishing a baccalaureate degree is a "sell or process further" decision.

## WRITING EXERCISE — Qualitative Factors in Decision Making

To emphasize that any decision encompasses qualitative, as well as quantitative, factors, ask your students to write an answer to one or more of the following questions (TM 25-8):

1.  A diversified food company is considering the closing of its condiment division. What qualitative factors should be considered before discontinuing a division or product line?

**Possible response:** Since the business is a diversified food company, closing a division could adversely affect the company's overall reputation as a full service provider. Divisions that are not profitable can still provide a benefit to the overall company by making other divisions more profitable.

2.  An automobile manufacturer has decided to allow outside suppliers to bid on all parts necessary to make its vehicles. What qualitative factors should be considered by management in deciding whether or not to turn over the production of a part to an outside supplier?

**Possible response**: When outside suppliers are considered to replace internal manufacturing, the company must consider the loss of control in supply and manufacturing specifications. Additional considerations might involve the ability to claim the automobile is 100% manufactured by the company.

3. What are the qualitative factors you might consider when determining whether or not to replace your car?

**Possible response**: One qualitative factor to consider is that you know the history of how your car was cared for versus the history of a replacement (used) car. An additional consideration is whether you like your car and if it provides you the functionality you require. Other qualitative factors might include the sentimental value of the existing car and whether a different car would provide a change and the excitement of something new and different.

# OBJECTIVE 2

**Determine the selling price of a product, using the product cost concept.**

## KEY TERMS

Product Cost Concept          Target Costing

## SUGGESTED APPROACH

The normal selling price of any product can be expressed using the following formula:

Normal Selling Price = Cost + Markup

The text presents three different techniques for determining the selling price of the product: the total cost, product cost, and variable cost concept. Emphasize that all three methods should lead a company to the same selling price. Therefore, selecting a method depends on how a company accumulates and reports product costs. This section describes the product cost concept. Total cost and variable cost methods are described in the Appendix. Use the following Demonstration Problem and Group Learning Activity to illustrate how product cost is used to set product prices.

## DEMONSTRATION PROBLEM — Product Cost Concept

B Squared Inc. uses the product cost concept of applying cost plus approach to product pricing. The costs of producing and selling 35,000 units of soccer balls are as follows:

Variable Cost per Unit:
Direct Materials          $ 4.00
Direct Labor              5.00

Factory Overhead          3.50
Selling and Admin        2.50
Total                    $16.00

Fixed Cost:
Factory Overhead        $100,000
Selling and Admin Exp.     45,000

B Squared desires a profit of equal to 20% of total assets of $400,000. Determine the selling price per ball.

**Solution:**

Total Manufacturing Cost:
Variable Cost ($12.50 × 35,000)$437,500
Fixed Cost                     100,000
Total                       $537,500

Cost per unit: $537,500/35,000 = $15.36

Markup Percentage = (Desired profit + Total Selling and Admin Expenses)/Total Manufacturing Cost
Markup Percentage = (80,000 + 45,000 + 87,500)/537,500 = .3953 or 40% rounded

Cost per unit             $15.36
Markup (15.36 × 40%)      6.14
Selling price             $21.50

## GROUP LEARNING ACTIVITY — Product Cost Concept

Some companies include only manufacturing costs in the cost reported for a product. In this case, the markup added to the product cost must compensate for selling and administrative expenses, as well as the desired level of profit. The product cost concept is well suited to manufacturers.

The formula to calculate the markup percentage under the product cost method is as follows:

Markup Percentage = <u>Desired Profit + Total Selling & Administrative Expenses</u>
Total Product Costs

Ask your students to calculate the selling price of the product described in TM 25-9 using the product cost and variable cost methods. The correct solution is shown on TM 25-10.

## INTERNET ACTIVITY — Target Costing

Have your students explore "Target Costing" by performing an Internet search. At the time this manual was written, the following Web site provided interesting information, including ten steps to install a comprehensive target cost approach: http://www.npd-solutions.com/target.html.

# OBJECTIVE 3

**Compute the relative profitability of products in bottleneck production processes.**

## KEY TERMS

Production Bottleneck          Theory of Constraints (TOC)

## SUGGESTED APPROACH

Students might not be familiar with the concepts of production constraints (bottlenecks). As a first step, demonstrate what bottlenecks are and how they impact production processes. After using the Demonstration Problem for this purpose, move on to the group learning activity and class discussion ideas.

## DEMONSTRATION PROBLEM — Simulating Production Constraints

Have five students line up in a row. Provide each student with two dice, except for the student in the third position, who gets one die. Place four poker chips between each student, representing work in process. The object of this exercise is to move poker chips from the beginning of the line to the end of the line. Poker chips are moved from beginning to end based on the roll of the dice.  For example, if a student's roll of the dice adds up to seven, he/she will attempt to move seven poker chips on to the next position. If the student doesn't have seven poker chips, he/she will move all of the chips in work in process to the next position. Have a stack of poker chips (representing raw materials) in front of the first position. Ask the students to roll the dice ten times on your count. When the simulation is finished, discuss the following questions:

1.  How many chips do you think were processed over the ten turns? (Have the output counted at this time.) Answer: On average, the complete line can only move as fast as the slowest operation. Thus, even though all positions, except position 3, have two dice, they do not add to throughput capacity. The average output is based on position 3. Since this position will roll an average of 3.5 per turn, over the ten turns, the expected output of the line is 35 chips.

2.  What happened between positions 2 and 3, and why? Answer: Poker chips stacked up in front of position 3. There is no place for these chips to go. Positions 1 and 2 are paced at an average roll of 7, since they have two dice. Position 3, with only one die, cannot keep up. As a result, chips pile up in front of position 3.

3.  Was the additional production from positions 1 and 2 "productive"? Answer: not really. These positions produced chips that cannot get through the line. If position 3 does not receive any more capacity, then these chips will never get fully processed. One of the concepts of the theory of constraints is that throughput only "counts" if the production results in sales. Throughput resulting in inventory is not value added. Thus, the extra dice of capacity in positions 1 and 2 is a wasted resource.

4. What is happening in positions 4 and 5? Answer: They are operating way below capacity. They are rolling averages of 7 but can only move averages of 3.5 chips. In other words, they are starved for work because position 3 operates at a much slower pace than do positions 4 and 5. The extra dice of capacity in positions 4 and 5 is waste. Clearly the chain is only as strong as the weakest link.

5. How can these problems be avoided? Answer: Naturally, the firm would want to remove the constraint at position 3 by purchasing another die. However, if this if not feasible, the theory of constraints suggests that the bottleneck should be the drumbeat for the rest of the line. Therefore, whatever position 3 rolls becomes the automatic roll for everybody else. In this way, the line becomes balanced to the constraining resource. Notice that this does not solve the problem of the wasted capacity in positions 1, 2, 4, and 5.

## GROUP LEARNING ACTIVITY — Product Profitability in Constrained Environments

Divide your class into groups. Provide each group with a copy of Handout 25-2. This handout is a problem where products must be processed through a bottleneck. Ask your students to answer the questions provided in the handout. The solution is provided on TMs 25-11 and 25-12.

# OBJECTIVE 4

Allocate product costs using activity-based costing.

## KEY TERMS

Activities                          Activity-Based Costing (ABC)
Activity Base                       Activity Rate

## SUGGESTED APPROACH

Activity-based costing helps in setting product prices by providing more accurate product costs. TM 25-11 illustrates the allocation of factory overhead in an activity-based costing (ABC) system. In an ABC system, management must identify all the activities necessary to manufacture a product. Factory overhead costs are first allocated to these activities. For example, one activity that absorbs factory overhead costs is machine setup. Under ABC, all costs incurred in setting up machines would be allocated to the setup activity. The illustration in TM 25-13 assumes a simple manufacturing process with only three activities.

Next, factory overhead is allocated to products based on the activities they consume in the manufacturing process. Continuing with the machine setup example, the cost of a setup would be calculated based on the total cost allocated to the setup activity and the total number of setups performed. This cost can then be allocated to a product based on the number of setups required to make the product.

As you cover ABC costing, you will need to stress the following points:

1. ABC changes only the way overhead costs are allocated.

2. When identifying the activities needed to manufacture their product, many companies find inefficiencies that they didn't know existed. These inefficiencies can be eliminated, reducing the product's cost.

3. ABC gained popularity because many manufacturing experts believed that traditional cost accounting "undercosted" complex products. Assigning too little cost to a product overstates its profit margin.

4. Many companies developed ABC systems independently of their cost accounting systems. In this case, ABC is used only for decision making. It is not used for inventory valuation or financial statements.

## LECTURE AID — The Need for ABC Costing

The following real-world example illustrates how traditional cost systems can understate the cost of complex products.

> A manufacturer of surgical gloves traditionally made gloves in one color: white. The company received a request from one of its customers to make each size glove a different color. The customer wanted small gloves to be pink, medium to be yellow, and large to be green.
>
> Every time the manufacturer would start to produce a colored glove, the machines would have to be shut down while colored dye was pumped into them. At the end of the production run, workers had to clean the machines to remove the remaining dye. The special setup and cleaning caused the company to spend more on labor to make the colored gloves.
>
> No matter how thoroughly the machines were cleaned after producing a colored glove, they still contained residue from the dye. To remove the residue, materials had to be run through the machine. So, a batch of gloves was made and scrapped just to prepare the machine to make white (or another color) gloves.
>
> The company allocated overhead based on machine hours. Since the white and colored gloves used exactly the same machine time while they were being made, they were assigned the same amount of overhead. As a result, the colored gloves were "undercosted" because they were clearly more expensive to produce.

Another example is two pen factories—one that sells only blue pens and one that sells pens of all colors. Both sell 100,000 pens per month. Assume you walk into the multicolor pen factory, but you're color blind. How would you know you are in the factory that makes a variety of pen colors? (Answer: There would be more activities than in the blue pen factory, such as color cleanouts, additional materials requisitions and purchasing, more quality checks and rework, etc.)

## DEMONSTRATION PROBLEM — ABC Costing

Allocating factory overhead to products under an ABC system can be explained as a four-step process.

**Step 1**—Identify activities: ABC costing allocates factory overhead to the activities that consume factory overhead costs. This forces a company to identify the activities necessary to make its product.

For example, assume that a manufacturing company identifies the following activities as necessary to make a product:

1. Order materials.
2. Receive and inspect materials.
3. Schedule production.
4. Set up machines to make the product.
5. Make the product.
6. Inspect the finished product.
7. Pack and ship the product to the customer.

**Step 2**—Allocate costs to the activities: The company would start this step by determining the factory overhead costs it incurs to order materials (the first activity). These costs would include such items as the salaries of the purchasing agent(s) and staff, supplies used by the purchasing department, and depreciation on office equipment used by the purchasing department. Assume that these costs total $80,000.

**Step 3**—Select a cost driver: A means to allocate the cost of each activity to the product must be chosen. This is known as selecting a cost driver. The cost driver for any activity should be the event that causes costs to be incurred. For example, placing an order causes purchasing costs to be incurred.

**Step 4**—Allocate costs of activities to the product, using the cost driver: Assume that the purchasing department places 10,000 orders per year. The cost to place an order is calculated as follows:

$$\text{Cost to place an order} \quad = \quad \frac{\$80,000}{10,000 \text{ orders}} = \quad \$8 \text{ per order}$$

If manufacturing a product causes the purchasing agent to place two orders for materials, the overhead cost allocated to that product is $16.

Once this process is complete for the purchasing activity, the same steps must be taken for the remaining activities. As a result, ABC is usually implemented only with the use of a computer programmed to do the many calculations required.

## WRITING EXERCISE — Activity-Based Costing

Ask your students to write an answer to the following question (TM 25-14):

     How does an activity-based costing system aid in setting product prices?

**Possible response**: Activity-based costing identifies and traces costs and expenses to activities and to specific products, providing an accurate basis for setting product prices.

# APPENDIX — TOTAL AND VARIABLE COST CONCEPTS TO SETTING NORMAL PRICE

## KEY TERMS

Total Cost Concept            Variable Cost Concept

## SUGGESTED APPROACH

The normal selling price of any product can be expressed using the following formula:

Normal Selling Price = Cost + Markup

The text presents three different techniques for determining the selling price of the product: the total cost, product cost, and variable cost concept. Remind students that all three methods should lead a company to the same selling price. Therefore, selecting a method depends on how a company accumulates and reports product costs.

## DEMONSTRATION PROBLEM — Total Cost Concept

The total cost concept is the most convenient method for determining a product's selling price if a company includes all manufacturing, selling, and administrative costs associated with the product in its reported cost. A markup is then added to achieve the firm's desired profit.

For example, assume that the following costs are incurred to make 10,000 units of a product (TM 25-9):

| | |
|---|---|
| Variable manufacturing costs | $5 per unit |
| Variable selling and administrative costs | $2 per unit |
| Fixed factory overhead costs | $80,000 |
| Fixed selling and administrative expenses | $30,000 |

Ask your students to calculate the total cost to make 10,000 units and the cost to make one unit. (Answers: total cost = $180,000; unit cost = $18)

Next, state that this company wishes to price the product so that a profit of $27,000 will be made if all 10,000 units are sold. The company can determine the markup percentage that will be necessary to achieve this profit using the following formula:

$$\text{Markup Percentage} = \frac{\text{Desired Profit}}{\text{Total Costs}} = \frac{\$27,000}{\$180,000} = 15\%$$

Ask your students to calculate the selling price of the product if it is marked up 15 percent above the total cost. (Answer: $18 × 1.15 = $20.70)

Point out that the total cost concept would be used mostly by merchandising businesses.

In other cases, companies use the concept of variable costing when reporting a product's cost. Under this concept, all variable costs from manufacturing, selling, and administrative activities are included in determining the product's reported cost. When variable costing is used, the markup added to the product cost must compensate for all fixed costs, as well as the desired level of profit.

The formula to calculate the markup percentage under the variable cost method is:

$$\text{Markup Percentage} = \frac{\text{Desired Profit} + \text{Total Fixed Costs}}{\text{Total Variable Costs}}$$

Ask your students to calculate the selling price of the product described in TM 25-9 using the variable cost method. The correct solution is shown on TM 25-15.

# Differential Analysis

1. Badonsky Manufacturing needs to obtain a gear-cutting machine, which can be purchased for $75,000. Badonsky estimates that repair, maintenance, insurance, and property tax expense will be $20,000 for the machine's five-year life. At the end of the machine's life, it will have no salvage value.

   As an alternative, Badonsky can lease the machine for five years for $18,000 per year. If the machine is leased, Badonsky is required to pay only for routine maintenance on the machine, which is estimated to be $8,000 over the machine's life. All other costs will be paid by the lessor. Prepare a differential analysis to determine whether Badonsky should purchase or lease the machine.

2. Grayson Enterprises currently manufactures part A-14, one of the component parts used to assemble the company's main product. Specialty Parts has offered to make part A-14 for $12.50 per unit.

   Grayson's per-unit cost to make part A-14 is $14.75, as follows:

   | | |
   |---|---|
   | Direct materials | $5.00 |
   | Direct labor | 6.00 |
   | Variable factory overhead | 1.75 |
   | Fixed factory overhead | 2.00 |

   None of Grayson's fixed overhead costs will be eliminated if the part is purchased. However, the plant space currently used to manufacture the part can be leased to another company for $30,000 per year. Assuming that Grayson needs 100,000 parts per year, should the company continue to make part A-14 or buy it?

3. Apple Valley Orchards sells apples for $15.00 per bushel. The company has considered processing some of its apples into apple butter. Each bushel of apples will yield two dozen jars of apple butter, which can be sold for $1.50 per jar. The additional cost to process the apples into apple butter is $0.75 per jar. Use differential analysis to determine whether Apple Valley Orchards should make the apple butter.

4. Gooding Foods makes Goody-Goody brand peanut butter. The cost to make each jar is $2.05 and consists of the following:

   | | |
   |---|---|
   | Direct materials | $1.00 |
   | Direct labor | 0.25 |
   | Variable factory overhead | 0.30 |
   | Fixed factory overhead | 0.50 |

   A grocery store chain wants to purchase a generic brand peanut butter from Gooding and is willing to pay $1.50 per jar. The generic peanut butter will be made using a different recipe, lowering the direct materials cost to $0.80 per jar. Gooding can produce this special order using excess capacity; therefore, fixed costs will not increase. Use differential analysis to determine whether Gooding should accept this special order.

# Profitability Analysis with Production Constraints

Bono Pasta Company makes three types of pasta: spaghetti, elbows, and shells. The production process involves mixing, extruding, and drying. The drying operation is a constraining resource in this operation. The contribution margins per unit for the three products are shown below.

|                            | Spaghetti | Elbows | Shells |
|----------------------------|-----------|--------|--------|
| Sales price per unit       | $25       | $30    | $35    |
| Variable cost per unit     | 15        | 18     | 20     |
| Contribution margin per unit | $10     | $12    | $15    |

The fixed costs are $100,000. The production volume and constraint usage information for the three products are:

|                            | Spaghetti | Elbows | Shells |
|----------------------------|-----------|--------|--------|
| Drying hours per unit      | 0.50      | 0.25   | 0.10   |
| Units produced (prior year)| 8,000     | 4,000  | 2,000  |

The following profitability report has been prepared for the prior year's sales levels:

|                     | Spaghetti | Elbows   | Shells  | Total     |
|---------------------|-----------|----------|---------|-----------|
| Units of production | 8,000     | 4,000    | 2,000   |           |
| Revenues            | $200,000  | $120,000 | $70,000 | $390,000  |
| Less variable costs | 120,000   | 72,000   | 40,000  | 232,000   |
| Contribution margin | 80,000    | 48,000   | 30,000  | $158,000  |
| Less fixed costs    |           |          |         | 100,000   |
| Profit              |           |          |         | $ 58,000  |

Required: Answer the following questions.

a.  Which product is the most profitable and should be emphasized in marketing efforts? Why?

b.  If, during the upcoming year, Bono reduced spaghetti production by 2,000 units and replaced the released capacity with the sale of shells, what would be the impact on total profitability (fill in the table below)?

|                     | Spaghetti | Elbows | Shells | Total   |
|---------------------|-----------|--------|--------|---------|
| Units of production | 6,000     |        |        |         |
| Revenues            |           |        |        |         |
| Less variable costs |           |        |        |         |
| Contribution margin |           |        |        |         |
| Less fixed costs    |           |        |        | 100,000 |
| Profit              |           |        |        |         |

c.  Determine the price for spaghetti that would make spaghetti equal to the profitability of shells.

# HOMEWORK CHART WITH LEARNING OUTCOMES TAGGING

| Problem | Learning Objective | Description | DIFFICULTY | BUSPROG Primary | ACBSP Primary | IMA Managerial Only | BLOOM'S | TIME | Spread-sheet |
|---|---|---|---|---|---|---|---|---|---|
| DQ25-1 | 25-1 | | Easy | Analytic | Incremental analysis | Decision Analysis | Knowledge | 5 min. | |
| DQ25-2 | 25-1 | | Easy | Analytic | Incremental analysis | Decision Analysis | Knowledge | 5 min. | |
| DQ25-3 | 25-1 | | Easy | Analytic | Incremental analysis | Decision Analysis | Knowledge | 5 min. | |
| DQ25-4 | 25-1 | | Easy | Analytic | Incremental analysis | Decision Analysis | Knowledge | 5 min. | |
| DQ25-5 | 25-1 | | Easy | Analytic | Incremental analysis | Decision Analysis | Knowledge | 5 min. | |
| DQ25-6 | 25-1 | | Easy | Analytic | Incremental analysis | Decision Analysis | Knowledge | 5 min. | |
| DQ25-7 | 25-1 | | Easy | Analytic | Incremental analysis | Decision Analysis | Knowledge | 5 min. | |
| DQ25-8 | 25-2 | | Easy | Analytic | Incremental analysis | Decision Analysis | Knowledge | 5 min. | |
| DQ25-9 | 25-2 | | Easy | Analytic | Incremental analysis | Decision Analysis | Knowledge | 5 min. | |
| DQ25-10 | 25-3 | | Easy | Analytic | Incremental analysis | Decision Analysis | Knowledge | 5 min. | |
| DQ25-11 | 25-4 | | Easy | Analytic | Incremental analysis | Decision Analysis | Knowledge | 5 min. | |
| PE25-1A | 25-1 | Lease or sell | Easy | Analytic | Incremental analysis | Decision Analysis | Application | 10 min. | |
| PE25-1B | 25-1 | Lease or sell | Easy | Analytic | Incremental analysis | Decision Analysis | Application | 10 min. | |
| PE25-2A | 25-1 | Discontinue a segment | Easy | Analytic | Incremental analysis | Decision Analysis | Application | 10 min. | |
| PE25-2B | 25-1 | Discontinue a segment | Easy | Analytic | Incremental analysis | Decision Analysis | Application | 10 min. | |
| PE25-3A | 25-1 | Make or buy | Easy | Analytic | Incremental analysis | Decision Analysis | Application | 10 min. | |
| PE25-3B | 25-1 | Make or buy | Easy | Analytic | Incremental analysis | Decision Analysis | Application | 10 min. | |
| PE25-4A | 25-1 | Replace equipment | Easy | Analytic | Incremental analysis | Decision Analysis | Application | 10 min. | |
| PE25-4B | 25-1 | Replace equipment | Easy | Analytic | Incremental analysis | Decision Analysis | Application | 10 min. | |
| PE25-5A | 25-1 | Process or sell | Easy | Analytic | Incremental analysis | Decision Analysis | Application | 10 min. | |
| PE25-5B | 25-1 | Process or sell | Easy | Analytic | Incremental analysis | Decision Analysis | Application | 10 min. | |
| PE25-6A | 25-1 | Accept business at special price | Easy | Analytic | Incremental analysis | Decision Analysis | Application | 10 min. | |
| PE25-6B | 25-1 | Accept business at special price | Easy | Analytic | Incremental analysis | Decision Analysis | Application | 10 min. | |
| PE25-7A | 25-2 | Product cost markup percentage | Easy | Analytic | Incremental analysis | Decision Analysis | Application | 10 min. | |
| PE25-7B | 25-2 | Product cost markup percentage | Easy | Analytic | Incremental analysis | Decision Analysis | Application | 10 min. | |
| PE25-8A | 25-3 | Bottleneck profit | Easy | Analytic | Incremental analysis | Decision Analysis | Application | 10 min. | |
| PE25-8B | 25-3 | Bottleneck profit | Easy | Analytic | Incremental analysis | Decision Analysis | Application | 10 min. | |
| PE25-9A | 25-4 | Activity-based costing | Easy | Analytic | Incremental analysis | Decision Analysis | Application | 10 min. | |
| PE25-9B | 25-4 | Activity-based costing | Easy | Analytic | Incremental analysis | Decision Analysis | Application | 10 min. | |
| Ex25-1 | 25-1 | Differential analysis for a lease or sell decision | Easy | Analytic | Incremental analysis | Decision Analysis | Application | 15 min. | |

| Problem | Learning Objective | Description | DIFFICULTY | BUSPROG Primary | ACBSP Primary | IMA Managerial Only | BLOOM'S | TIME | Spread-sheet |
|---|---|---|---|---|---|---|---|---|---|
| Ex25-2 | 25-1 | Differential analysis for a lease or buy decision | Easy | Analytic | Incremental analysis | Decision Analysis | Application | 15 min. | |
| Ex25-3 | 25-1 | Differential analysis for a discontinued product | Easy | Analytic | Incremental analysis | Decision Analysis | Application | 15 min. | |
| Ex25-4 | 25-1 | Differential analysis for a discontinued product | Easy | Analytic | Incremental analysis | Decision Analysis | Application | 15 min. | X |
| Ex25-5 | 25-1 | Segment analysis, Charles Schwab Corporation | Moderate | Analytic | Incremental analysis | Decision Analysis | Application | 20 min. | |
| Ex25-6 | 25-1 | Decision to discontinue a product | Moderate | Analytic | Incremental analysis | Decision Analysis | Application | 15 min. | |
| Ex25-7 | 25-1 | Make-or-buy decision | Easy | Analytic | Incremental analysis | Decision Analysis | Application | 15 min. | X |
| Ex25-8 | 25-1 | Make-or-buy decision | Moderate | Analytic | Incremental analysis | Decision Analysis | Application | 30 min. | X |
| Ex25-9 | 25-1 | Machine replacement decision | Easy | Analytic | Incremental analysis | Decision Analysis | Application | 15 min. | |
| Ex25-10 | 25-1 | Differential analysis for machine replacement | Moderate | Analytic | Incremental analysis | Decision Analysis | Application | 20 min. | X |
| Ex25-11 | 25-1 | Sell or process further | Easy | Analytic | Incremental analysis | Decision Analysis | Application | 15 min. | |
| Ex25-12 | 25-1 | Sell or process further | Moderate | Analytic | Incremental analysis | Decision Analysis | Application | 20 min. | X |
| Ex25-13 | 25-1 | Decision on accepting additional business | Moderate | Analytic | Incremental analysis | Decision Analysis | Application | 20 min. | |
| Ex25-14 | 25-1 | Accepting business at a special price | Easy | Analytic | Incremental analysis | Decision Analysis | Application | 15 min. | |
| Ex25-15 | 25-1 | Decision on accepting additional business | Moderate | Analytic | Incremental analysis | Decision Analysis | Application | 20 min. | X |
| Ex25-16 | 25-2 | Product cost concept of product pricing | Moderate | Analytic | Incremental analysis | Decision Analysis | Application | 20 min. | |
| Ex25-17 | 25-2 | Product cost concept of product pricing | Moderate | Analytic | Incremental analysis | Decision Analysis | Application | 20 min. | |
| Ex25-18 | 25-2 | Target costing | Easy | Analytic | Incremental analysis | Decision Analysis | Application | 15 min. | |
| Ex25-19 | 25-2 | Target costing | Moderate | Analytic | Incremental analysis | Decision Analysis | Application | 30 min. | |
| Ex25-20 | 25-3 | Product decisions under bottlenecked operations | Moderate | Analytic | Incremental analysis | Decision Analysis | Application | 20 min. | |
| Ex25-21 | 25-3 | Product decisions under bottlenecked operations | Moderate | Analytic | Incremental analysis | Decision Analysis | Application | 20 min. | |
| Ex25-22 | 25-4 | Activity-based costing | Moderate | Analytic | Incremental analysis | Decision Analysis | Application | 30 min. | X |
| Ex25-23 | 25-4 | Activity-based costing | Moderate | Analytic | Incremental analysis | Decision Analysis | Application | 30 min. | |

| Problem | Learning Objective | Description | DIFFICULTY | BUSPROG Primary | ACBSP Primary | IMA Managerial Only | BLOOM'S | TIME | Spread-sheet |
|---|---|---|---|---|---|---|---|---|---|
| Ex25-24 | 25-4 | Activity rates and product costs using activity-based costing | Moderate | Analytic | Incremental analysis | Decision Analysis | Application | 30 min. | |
| Ex25-25 | Appendix | Total cost concept of product pricing | Moderate | Analytic | Incremental analysis | Decision Analysis | Application | 30 min. | |
| Ex25-26 | Appendix | Variable cost concept of product pricing | Moderate | Analytic | Incremental analysis | Decision Analysis | Application | 20 min. | |
| Pr25-1A | 25-1 | Differential analysis involving opportunity costs | Moderate | Analytic | Incremental analysis | Decision Analysis | Application | 45 min. | X |
| Pr25-2A | 25-1 | Differential analysis for machine replacement proposal | Moderate | Analytic | Incremental analysis | Decision Analysis | Application | 1 hour | X |
| Pr25-3A | 25-1 | Differential analysis for sales promotion proposal | Moderate | Analytic | Incremental analysis | Decision Analysis | Application | 1 hour | X |
| Pr25-4A | 25-1 | Differential analysis for further processing | Moderate | Analytic | Incremental analysis | Decision Analysis | Application | 45 min. | |
| Pr25-5A | 25-1, 25-2, Appendix | Product pricing using the cost-plus approach concepts; differential analysis for accepting additional business | Moderate | Analytic | Incremental analysis | Decision Analysis | Application | 1.5 hours | |
| Pr25-6A | 25-3 | Product pricing and profit analysis with bottleneck operations | Challenging | Analytic | Incremental analysis | Decision Analysis | Application | 1.5 hours | X |
| Pr25-7A | 25-4 | Activity-based costing | Challenging | Analytic | Incremental analysis | Decision Analysis | Application | 1.5 hours | X |
| Pr25-1B | 25-1 | Differential analysis involving opportunity costs | Challenging | Analytic | Incremental analysis | Decision Analysis | Application | 45 min. | X |
| Pr25-2B | 25-1 | Differential analysis for machine replacement proposal | Moderate | Analytic | Incremental analysis | Decision Analysis | Application | 1 hour | X |
| Pr25-3B | 25-1 | Differential analysis for sales promotion proposal | Moderate | Analytic | Incremental analysis | Decision Analysis | Application | 1 hour | |
| Pr25-4B | 25-1 | Differential analysis for further processing | Moderate | Analytic | Incremental analysis | Decision Analysis | Application | 45 min. | |
| Pr25-5B | 25-1, 25-2, Appendix | Product pricing using the cost-plus approach concepts; differential analysis for accepting additional business | Moderate | Analytic | Incremental analysis | Decision Analysis | Application | 1.5 hours | |
| Pr25-6B | 25-3 | Product pricing and profit analysis with bottleneck operations | Challenging | Analytic | Incremental analysis | Decision Analysis | Application | 1.5 hours | X |
| Pr25-7B | 25-4 | Activity-based costing | Challenging | Analytic | Incremental analysis | Decision Analysis | Application | 1.5 hours | X |

| Problem | Learning Objective | Description | DIFFICULTY | BUSPROG Primary | ACBSP Primary | IMA Managerial Only | BLOOM'S | TIME | Spread-sheet |
|---|---|---|---|---|---|---|---|---|---|
| CP25-1 | 25-1 | Product pricing | Challenging | Analytic | Incremental analysis | Decision Analysis | Analysis | 15 min. | |
| CP25-2 | 25-1 | Decision on accepting additional business | Easy | Ethics | Incremental analysis | Decision Analysis | Application | 15 min. | |
| CP25-3 | 25-1 | Accept business at a special price | Easy | Analytic | Incremental analysis | Decision Analysis | Application | 30 min. | |
| CP25-4 | 25-2 | Cost-plus and target costing concepts | Moderate | Analytic | Incremental analysis | Decision Analysis | Analysis | 30 min. | |
| CP25-5 | Appendix | Pricing decisions and markup on variable costs | Moderate | Analytic | Incremental analysis | Decision Analysis | Application | 1.5 hours | |
| CP25-6 | 25-4 | Identifying product cost distortion | Moderate | Analytic | Incremental analysis | Decision Analysis | Application | 1.5 hours | |

# Capital Investment Analysis

## OPENING COMMENTS

Capital investment analysis is a topic that usually receives detailed coverage in introductory finance courses and/or intermediate accounting. The purpose of this chapter is to give students a brief introduction to the basics of capital investment analysis using the following methods: average rate of return, cash payback, net present value, and internal rate of return.

Although accounting and finance may be treated as two distinct disciplines in academia, there is no clear dividing line in today's business world. Accountants must understand principles of finance in order to analyze company performance and make recommendations to management. Capital investment analysis is one of the most important techniques used to plan and control expenditures for fixed assets.

After studying the chapter, your students should be able to:

1. Explain the nature and importance of capital investment analysis.

2. Evaluate capital investment proposals using the average rate of return and cash payback methods.

3. Evaluate capital investment proposals using the net present value and internal rate of return methods.

4. List and describe factors that complicate capital investment analysis.

5. Diagram the capital rationing process.

# STUDENT FAQS

- Why does capital investment seem to be so important and affect several years?

- Which method of evaluating capital investment is the best to use?

- Should we apply all formulas used in this chapter, then evaluate from there? Or should we just use present value method?

- How does management decide the minimum rate of return in capital investment?

- Which factors complicate capital investment analysis?

# OBJECTIVE 1

**Explain the nature and importance of capital investment analysis.**

## KEY TERMS

Capital Investment Analysis     Time Value of Money Concept

## SUGGESTED APPROACH

Capital investment analysis is the process by which management plans, evaluates, and controls investments in fixed assets. Explain that capital investment decisions are some of the most important decisions made by management because they (1) frequently involve large sums of money and (2) affect operations for many years. Students can view the costs they spend in attending college as a capital investment in their careers.

# OBJECTIVE 2

**Evaluate capital investment proposals using the average rate of return and cash payback methods.**

## KEY TERMS

Average Rate of Return     Cash Payback Period

## SUGGESTED APPROACH

The text presents four methods of evaluating investment proposals. Data on two potential capital investments follow (Transparency Master [TM] 26-1). Use these data to illustrate the various methods of investment analysis:

|  | Project A | Project B |
|---|---|---|
| Cost | $560,000 | $900,000 |
| Expected life | 4 years | 4 years |
| Expected residual value | $0 | $0 |

| Expected Returns | Project A | | Project B | |
|---|---|---|---|---|
|  | Income | Net Cash Flow | Income | Net Cash Flow |
| Year 1 | $10,000 | $150,000 | $100,000 | $325,000 |
| Year 2 | 50,000 | 190,000 | 100,000 | 325,000 |
| Year 3 | 80,000 | 220,000 | 100,000 | 325,000 |
| Year 4 | 84,000 | 224,000 | 100,000 | 325,000 |

Stress that the difference between the annual income and annual cash flows from each project is the depreciation expense ($140,000 per year for Project A and $225,000 per year for Project B using straight-line depreciation and ignoring the effect of income taxes).

## DEMONSTRATION PROBLEM — Average Rate of Return

Average rate of return measures the profitability of an investment. The formula for average rate of return is as follows:

$$\text{Average Rate of Return} = \frac{\text{Estimated Average Annual Income}}{\text{Average Investment}}$$

Demonstrate the average rate of return for Project A as follows:

$$\text{Estimated Average Annual Income} = \frac{\$10,000 + \$50,000 + \$80,000 + \$84,000}{4}$$

$$= \$56,000$$

$$\text{Average Investment} = \frac{\$560,000 + 0}{2} = \$280,000$$

$$\text{Average Rate of Return} = \frac{\$56,000}{\$280,000} = 20\%$$

Ask your students to calculate the average rate of return for Project B and write the answer in their notes (Answer: $100,000/$450,000 = 22%).

## DEMONSTRATION PROBLEM — Cash Payback Method

Explain that the cash payback period is the amount of time (in years) it takes to recover the cash invested in a project. A project's annual cash flows are used to determine the cash payback period.

For example, the cash payback period for Project A would be calculated as follows:

|        | Annual Cash Flow | Cumulative Cash Flow |
|--------|------------------|----------------------|
| Year 1 | $150,000         | $150,000             |
| Year 2 | 190,000          | 340,000              |
| Year 3 | 220,000          | 560,000              |

The $560,000 investment is recovered in three years.

Ask your students to calculate the payback period for Project B and write it in their notes. (Answer: $900,000/325,000 = 2.8 yrs.)

# OBJECTIVE 3

**Evaluate capital investment proposals using the net present value and internal rate of return methods.**

## KEY TERMS

Annuity
Internal Rate of Return (IRR) Method
Net Present Value Method

Present Value Concept
Present Value Index
Present Value of an Annuity

## GROUP LEARNING ACTIVITY — Present Value Concepts

Prior to covering the net present value and internal rate of return methods of evaluating capital investments, you may want to briefly review present value concepts. These concepts were introduced in Chapter 14 when covering the accounting for bonds.

TM 26-2 presents a few short present value problems. Ask your students to work in groups to answer these questions. Their level of success with this activity will allow you to assess how much review they need. Remind students that abbreviated present value tables can be found in Exhibits 1 and 2 in the text. More complete tables are found in Appendix A at the end of the text. The solution to this assignment is displayed on TM 26-3.

# DEMONSTRATION PROBLEM — Net Present Value

Under the net present value method, the present values of the cash flows from a project are compared to the amount that must be invested in the project.

For example, assume the company considering Projects A and B wants a 15 percent return on any investment. The present value of Project A's cash flows would be determined using the present value table in Exhibit 1 of the text, as follows:

|        | Cash Flow | Present Value Factor | Present Value of Project's Cash Flows |
|--------|-----------|----------------------|----------------------------------------|
| Year 1 | $150,000  | .870                 | $130,500                               |
| Year 2 | 190,000   | .756                 | 143,640                                |
| Year 3 | 220,000   | .658                 | 144,760                                |
| Year 4 | 224,000   | .572                 | 128,128                                |
|        |           | Total                | $547,028                               |
|        |           | Amount to be invested | 560,000                               |
|        |           | Net present value    | $ (12,972)                             |

Because the net present value of this project is negative, its cash flows are not providing the minimum 15 percent return required by the company. Therefore, the project should be rejected.

Ask your students to determine the net present value of Project B and write it in their notes. Remind them that Project B has equal cash flow amounts in each of the four years of the project. Therefore, it may be valued as an annuity using the present value table in Exhibit 2 of the text. After giving your students a couple of minutes to work, review the following calculations:

| Annual Cash Flow | Present Value Factor—Annuity | Present Value of Project's Cash Flows |
|------------------|------------------------------|----------------------------------------|
| $325,000         | 2.855                        | $927,875                               |
|                  | Amount to be invested        | 900,000                                |
|                  | Net present value            | $ 27,875                               |

Because the net present value of this project is positive, it is providing a return above 15 percent. Therefore, the company should invest in project B.

Your students may find the following notation useful:

If NPV > 0, invest
If NPV = 0, invest          where NPV = net present value
If NPV < 0, reject

# WRITING EXERCISE — Minimum Rate of Return

Ask your students to write an answer to the following question (TM 26-4):

> What are some of the factors that management would consider in setting the minimum rate of return for investments?

**Possible response**: In setting the rate of return on investments, management should consider the market rate of return expected by investing in similar available opportunities. Additionally, management should assess the risk involved among the various options. Management should also assess the long term needs of the business in relation to projected sales. Improved technology may lead to savings in manufacturing cost, providing a competitive advantage.

You can use this writing exercise to stimulate a discussion on the cost of capital and the relationship between risk and return.

# DEMONSTRATION PROBLEM — Present Value Index

TM 26-5 presents six investment alternatives. Under Case I, you will find the net present values for three projects that all require the same initial investment. If a company evaluating these projects could invest in only one, it should choose the project with the highest net present value.

Under Case II, each project requires a different initial investment. Therefore, a present value index is helpful in choosing the most attractive investment from this group. Ask your students to calculate the present value index for each project using the following formula:

$$\text{Present Value Index} = \frac{\text{Total Present Value of Net Cash Flows}}{\text{Amount to be Invested}}$$

The correct present value indexes are shown on TM 26-6. Stress that Project B has the highest net present value but the lowest net present value index. This occurs because of the relatively high investment required by Project B.

# DEMONSTRATION PROBLEM — Internal Rate of Return

Internal rate of return (IRR) uses present value concepts to determine the rate earned on an investment. Under the internal rate of return method, students "work backwards" to find the discount rate where a project's net present value is zero. For projects that have cash flows that vary from year to year, the internal rate of return must be found through trial and error.

For example, you previously demonstrated that the return on Project A (from TM 26-1) is less than 15 percent, because the project's net present value was negative when discounted at 15 percent. Ask your students to determine the net present value of the project using a 12 percent discount rate. After allowing a couple of minutes for them to work, share the following calculation:

|  | Cash Flow | Present Value Factor | Present Value of Project's Cash Flows |
|---|---|---|---|
| Year 1 | $150,000 | .893 | $133,950 |
| Year 2 | 190,000 | .797 | 151,430 |
| Year 3 | 220,000 | .712 | 156,640 |
| Year 4 | 224,000 | .636 | 142,464 |
|  |  | Total | $584,484 |
|  |  | Amount to be invested | 560,000 |
|  |  | Net present value | $ 24,484 |

Because the net present value of Project A is positive when discounted at 12 percent, its rate of return is greater than 12 percent. Therefore, you can conclude that Project A's internal rate of return is between 12 and 15 percent.

With the present value table in text Exhibit 1, that is as close as you can get in estimating Project A's internal rate of return. This range could be narrowed using a present value table that contains more interest rate possibilities, a computer, or a calculator that includes present value capabilities.

If a project provides equal cash flows in each year of its life (an annuity), internal rate of return may be calculated without using a trial and error process.

For example, Project B costs $900,000 and has cash flows of $325,000 per year. Previous calculations showed that Project B's internal rate of return is higher than 15 percent, because it has a positive net present value when discounted at 15 percent. The net present value of Project B is zero when it is discounted at its internal rate of return. Project B's net present value is zero when the total present value of its cash flows equals the project's initial investment of $900,000.

Therefore, if

$$\frac{\text{Annual Net}}{\text{Cash Flow}} \times \frac{\text{Present Value Factor}}{\text{for an Annuity}} = \frac{\text{Present Value of}}{\text{Project's Cash Flows}}$$

then

$$\text{Present Value Factor for an Annuity} = \frac{\text{Present Value of Project's Cash Flows}}{\text{Annual Net Cash Flow}}$$

Using data from Project B:

$$\text{Present Value Factor for an Annuity} = \frac{\$900,000}{\$325,000} = 2.769$$

Because Project B has a four-year life, look at the four-year row on the present value table in text Exhibit 2. Because 2.769 is between 2.855 (15 percent) and 2.589 (20 percent), the internal rate of return is between 15 and 20 percent.

## LECTURE AID — Comparing Methods to Evaluate Capital Investments

TMs 26-7 and 26-8 summarize the advantages and disadvantages of these four methods of evaluating capital investments. As you review this TM, emphasize that non-present value methods are often used to screen proposals. They also are appropriate for investments that have short lives.

# OBJECTIVE 4

List and describe factors that complicate capital investment analysis.

## KEY TERMS

Currency Exchange Rate        Inflation

## SUGGESTED APPROACH

Remind students that Chapter 26 is only an introduction to capital budgeting. The factors that complicate capital budgeting, which were ignored in previous examples, include income taxes; the effect of unequal proposal lives; the possibility of leasing, rather than purchasing, assets; uncertainty related to cash flows and interest rates; and changes in price levels due to inflation.

Emphasize that capital investment analysis uses estimates of future costs to make decisions. In response to the uncertainties of estimates, including the impact of inflation, many accountants perform sensitivity analyses using microcomputers. Such analyses can examine the impact of varying different assumptions about future revenues, costs, investment life, or inflation.

Because income taxes can have a profound influence on capital investment analysis, you may want to share an example of their impact using the following demonstration problem.

## DEMONSTRATION PROBLEM — Income Taxes in Capital Investment Analysis

TM 26-1 presented two projects that were used to illustrate capital investment analysis. Some of the relevant information from Project A is recapped as follows:

Cost: $560,000
Life: 4 years
Depreciation per year: $140,000 (straight line)
Net cash flow—year 1: $150,000
Net income—year 1: $10,000

The difference between the project's net cash flow and net income was explained as the yearly depreciation charge, which is a noncash expense.

Income taxes were ignored in this example. In reality, the $150,000 net cash flow was a pre-tax net cash flow. To show the cash flows on an after-tax basis, income taxes must be subtracted.

Assume that this company was in a 30 percent tax bracket. The after-tax net cash flows would be calculated as follows:

Taxes paid (based on the company's net income):
$10,000 × 30% = $3,000

After-tax net cash flow:

| | |
|---|---:|
| Before-tax net cash flow | $150,000 |
| Less taxes paid | 3,000 |
| | $147,000 |

Using the after-tax cash flow in a net present value analysis yields a more accurate answer.

Emphasize that depreciation is deductible for tax purposes. Therefore, the company pays taxes on its net income, not its net cash flow. Because taxes would have been $45,000 without this deduction ($150,000 × 30% = $45,000), the depreciation deduction saves $42,000 in taxes ($140,000 × 30%).

## LECTURE AID — Qualitative Factors in Evaluating Capital Investments

Capital investment decisions must consider qualitative factors in addition to quantitative analysis. The group learning activity under Objective 5 will provide your students with an opportunity to consider qualitative factors in choosing between investment alternatives.

TM 26-9 lists several qualitative factors that are important in today's technology driven manufacturing environment. The "competitive squeeze" felt by many companies is forcing business to look beyond the numbers and consider investments based on their ability to help the firm compete in a global marketplace. TM 26-9 lists many of the important qualitative issues to consider before investing in factory automation.

# OBJECTIVE 5

**Diagram the capital rationing process.**

## KEY TERM

Capital Rationing

## SUGGESTED APPROACH

Capital rationing occurs whenever limited funds force management to choose only a few of the capital investment projects under consideration. The capital rationing process is outlined on TM 26-10. Review this TM with your class.

The following group learning activity asks students to apply the concepts of capital rationing. It will also review the four methods for evaluating capital investment projects that were illustrated earlier in the chapter and the qualitative factors affecting a capital investment decision.

## GROUP LEARNING ACTIVITY — Capital Rationing

Handout 26-1 is a capital rationing problem. It asks your students to evaluate five capital budgeting proposals. These proposals are to be ranked in the order they should be funded based on each project's net present value, internal rate of return, and qualitative value to the company. Average rate of return and cash payback period are used to screen the five proposals.

Distribute this handout to your class and instruct students to work the problem in small groups. The solution to the quantitative analysis is shown on TM 26-11. Take time to discuss the qualitative issues and your students' final rankings in class.

## Capital Rationing

Plasticon manufactures plastic containers used to package a variety of liquid consumer products (such as fabric softener, cleaners, shampoo, hair spray, and liquid soap). The containers are manufactured on a job-order basis to customer specifications.

Plasticon has received five proposals for capital investment projects. Your job is to evaluate these proposals and rank them in the order in which they should be funded. Begin your analysis by computing the average rate of return and cash payback period for each proposal. Any project that has an average rate of return of less than 15 percent or a cash payback period of longer than five years should be eliminated from further consideration. After this initial screening, compute the net present value (using a 15 percent discount rate) and internal rate of return for the remaining projects. Rank the projects based on both their profitability and overall merit to the corporation (qualitative factors).

| Projects: | A | B | C | D | E |
|---|---|---|---|---|---|
| Cost | $200,000 | $250,000 | $325,000 | $500,000 | $400,000 |
| Life (in years) | 8 | 10 | 10 | 10 | 8 |
| Residual value | $0 | $0 | $0 | $0 | $0 |
| Annual project income | $17,000 | $18,000 | $33,000 | $55,000 | $45,000 |
| Annual net cash flows | $42,000 | $43,000 | $65,500 | $105,000 | $95,000 |

Project A: This proposal requests funds to purchase hardware and software that will allow the accounting department to process payroll in-house. Paychecks are currently processed by an outside payroll service company. The annual increase in net income and cash flows will result from cost savings if the payroll function is no longer contracted to an outside company.

Project B: This proposal requests funds for new manufacturing equipment. This equipment will allow Plasticon to make containers as large as ten gallons. Currently, Plasticon can not make containers that are larger than three gallons.

Project C: This proposal requests funds for equipment to make stick-on labels that are applied to the plastic containers. Currently, all stick-on labels are ordered from another company. This supplier has not proven very reliable in meeting delivery deadlines.

Project D: This proposal requests funds for automated manufacturing equipment that will reduce the cycle time from receipt of a customer order to delivery of that order. Plasticon's cycle time is currently seven days. The automated equipment will reduce that time to four days while saving costs due to the elimination of five jobs. It will also make Plasticon more competitive; the company's major competitor currently has a cycle time of five days.

Project E: This proposal requests funds for computerized drafting and design equipment that will allow engineers to complete manufacturing instructions on special orders more quickly. This equipment should reduce Plasticon's cycle time from seven to five days.

| Present Value of an Annuity of $1 at Compound Interest | | | | | | | |
|---|---|---|---|---|---|---|---|
| Period | 12% | 13% | 14% | 15% | 16% | 17% | 18% |
| 8 | 4.968 | 4.799 | 4.639 | 4.487 | 4.344 | 4.207 | 4.078 |
| 10 | 5.650 | 5.426 | 5.216 | 5.019 | 4.833 | 4.659 | 4.494 |

# HOMEWORK CHART WITH LEARNING OUTCOMES TAGGING

| Problem | Learning Objective | Description | DIFFICULTY | BUSPROG Primary | ACBSP Primary | ACBSP Secondary | IMA Managerial Only | BLOOM'S | TIME | Spread-sheet |
|---|---|---|---|---|---|---|---|---|---|---|
| DQ26-1 | 26-1 | | Easy | Analytic | Payback/ARR Methods | | Investment Decisions | Knowledge | 5 min. | |
| DQ26-2 | 26-2 | | Easy | Analytic | Payback/ARR Methods | | Investment Decisions | Knowledge | 5 min. | |
| DQ26-3 | 26-2 | | Easy | Analytic | Payback/ARR Methods | | Investment Decisions | Knowledge | 5 min. | |
| DQ26-4 | 26-2 | | Easy | Analytic | Payback/ARR Methods | | Investment Decisions | Knowledge | 5 min. | |
| DQ26-5 | 26-2 | | Easy | Analytic | Payback/ARR Methods | | Investment Decisions | Knowledge | 5 min. | |
| DQ26-6 | 26-2 | | Easy | Analytic | NPV/IRR Methods | | Investment Decisions | Knowledge | 5 min. | |
| DQ26-7 | 26-2 | | Easy | Analytic | NPV/IRR Methods | | Investment Decisions | Knowledge | 5 min. | |
| DQ26-8 | 26-2 | | Easy | Analytic | NPV/IRR Methods | | Investment Decisions | Knowledge | 5 min. | |
| DQ26-9 | 26-2 | | Easy | Analytic | NPV/IRR Methods | | Investment Decisions | Knowledge | 5 min. | |
| DQ26-10 | 26-2 | | Easy | Analytic | NPV/IRR Methods | | Investment Decisions | Knowledge | 5 min. | |
| DQ26-11 | 26-3 | | Easy | Analytic | NPV/IRR Methods | | Investment Decisions | Knowledge | 5 min. | |
| DQ26-12 | 26-4 | | Easy | Analytic | NPV/IRR Methods | | Investment Decisions | Knowledge | 5 min. | |
| PE26-1A | 26-2 | Average rate of return | Easy | Analytic | Payback/ARR Methods | | Investment Decisions | Application | 5 min. | |
| PE26-1B | 26-2 | Average rate of return | Easy | Analytic | Payback/ARR Methods | | Investment Decisions | Application | 5 min. | |
| PE26-2A | 26-2 | Cash payback period | Easy | Analytic | Payback/ARR Methods | | Investment Decisions | Application | 5 min. | |
| PE26-2B | 26-2 | Cash payback period | Easy | Analytic | Payback/ARR Methods | | Investment Decisions | Application | 5 min. | |
| PE26-3A | 26-3 | Net present value | Easy | Analytic | NPV/IRR Methods | | Investment Decisions | Application | 5 min. | |
| PE26-3B | 26-3 | Net present value | Easy | Analytic | NPV/IRR Methods | | Investment Decisions | Application | 10 min. | |

| Problem | Learning Objective | Description | DIFFICULTY | BUSPROG Primary | ACBSP Primary | ACBSP Secondary | IMA Managerial Only | BLOOM'S | TIME | Spread-sheet |
|---|---|---|---|---|---|---|---|---|---|---|
| PE26-4A | 26-3 | Internal rate of return | Easy | Analytic | NPV/IRR Methods | | Investment Decisions | Application | 10 min. | |
| PE26-4B | 26-3 | Internal rate of return | Easy | Analytic | NPV/IRR Methods | | Investment Decisions | Application | 5 min. | |
| PE26-5A | 26-4 | Net present value—unequal lives | Easy | Analytic | NPV/IRR Methods | | Investment Decisions | Application | 10 min. | |
| PE26-5B | 26-4 | Net present value—unequal lives | Easy | Analytic | NPV/IRR Methods | | Investment Decisions | Application | 10 min. | |
| Ex26-1 | 26-2 | Average rate of return | Easy | Analytic | Payback/ARR Methods | | Investment Decisions | Application | 10 min. | |
| Ex26-2 | 26-2 | Average rate of return— cost savings | Easy | Analytic | Payback/ARR Methods | | Investment Decisions | Application | 10 min. | |
| Ex26-3 | 26-2 | Average rate of return—new product | Easy | Analytic | Payback/ARR Methods | | Investment Decisions | Application | 10 min. | |
| Ex26-4 | 26-2 | Calculate cash flows | Easy | Analytic | Payback/ARR Methods | | Investment Decisions | Application | 10 min. | |
| Ex26-5 | 26-2 | Cash payback period | Easy | Analytic | Payback/ARR Methods | | Investment Decisions | Application | 15 min. | |
| Ex26-6 | 26-2 | Cash payback method | Easy | Analytic | Payback/ARR Methods | | Investment Decisions | Application | 15 min. | X |
| Ex26-7 | 26-3 | Net present value method | Easy | Analytic | NPV/IRR Methods | | Investment Decisions | Application | 15 min. | |
| Ex26-8 | 26-3 | Net present value method | Moderate | Analytic | NPV/IRR Methods | | Investment Decisions | Application | 20 min. | |
| Ex26-9 | 26-3 | Net present value method-annuity | Moderate | Analytic | NPV/IRR Methods | | Investment Decisions | Application | 20 min. | |
| Ex26-10 | 26-3 | Net present value method-annuity | Moderate | Analytic | NPV/IRR Methods | | Investment Decisions | Application | 20 min. | |
| Ex26-11 | 26-3 | Net present value method | Moderate | Analytic | NPV/IRR Methods | | Investment Decisions | Application | 30 min. | |
| Ex26-12 | 26-3 | Present value index | Easy | Analytic | NPV/IRR Methods | | Investment Decisions | Application | 15 min. | |
| Ex26-13 | 26-3 | Net present value method and present value index | Moderate | Analytic | NPV/IRR Methods | | Investment Decisions | Application | 20 min. | |
| Ex26-14 | 26-2, 26-3 | Average rate of return, cash payback period, net present value method | Moderate | Analytic | NPV/IRR Methods | | Investment Decisions | Application | 20 min. | |

| Problem | Learning Objective | Description | DIFFICULTY | BUSPROG Primary | ACBSP Primary | ACBSP Secondary | IMA Managerial Only | BLOOM'S | TIME | Spread-sheet |
|---|---|---|---|---|---|---|---|---|---|---|
| Ex26-15 | 26-2, 26-3, 26-4 | Payback period, net present value analysis, and qualitative considerations | Easy | Analytic | NPV/IRR Methods | | Investment Decisions | Application | 15 min. | |
| Ex26-16 | 26-3 | Internal rate of return method | Easy | Analytic | NPV/IRR Methods | | Investment Decisions | Application | 15 min. | |
| Ex26-17 | 26-3, 26-4 | Internal rate of return method | Easy | Analytic | NPV/IRR Methods | | Investment Decisions | Application | 10 min. | |
| Ex26-18 | 26-3 | Internal rate of return method- two projects | Easy | Analytic | NPV/IRR Methods | | Investment Decisions | Application | 15 min. | |
| Ex26-19 | 26-3 | Net present value method and internal rate of return method | Moderate | Analytic | NPV/IRR Methods | | Investment Decisions | Application | 20 min. | |
| Ex26-20 | 26-3 | Identify error in capital investment analysis calculations | Easy | Analytic | NPV/IRR Methods | | Investment Decisions | Application | 10 min. | |
| Ex26-21 | 26-3, 26-4 | Net present value-unequal lines | Moderate | Analytic | NPV/IRR Methods | | Investment Decisions | Application | 20 min. | X |
| Ex26-22 | 26-3, 26-4 | Net present value-unequal lines | Easy | Analytic | NPV/IRR Methods | | Investment Decisions | Application | 10 min. | |
| Pr26-1A | 26-2, 26-3 | Average rate of return method, net present value method, and analysis | Moderate | Analytic | Payback/ARR Methods | NPV/IRR Methods | Investment Decisions | Application | 1.5 hours | X |
| Pr26-2A | 26-2, 26-3 | Cash payback period, net present value method, and analysis | Moderate | Analytic | Payback/ARR Methods | NPV/IRR Methods | Investment Decisions | Application | 1.5 hours | X |
| Pr26-3A | 26-3 | Net present value method, present value index, and analysis | Moderate | Analytic | Payback/ARR Methods | NPV/IRR Methods | Investment Decisions | Application | 1 hour | X |
| Pr26-4A | 26-3 | Net present value method, internal rate of return method, and analysis | Moderate | Analytic | NPV/IRR Methods | | Investment Decisions | Application | 1.5 hours | |
| Pr26-5A | 26-3, 26-4 | Evaluate alternative capital investment decisions | Moderate | Analytic | NPV/IRR Methods | | Investment Decisions | Application | 1.5 hours | X |
| Pr26-6A | 26-2, 26-3, 26-5 | Capital rationing decision involving four proposals | Challenging | Analytic | Payback/ARR Methods | NPV/IRR Methods | Investment Decisions | Application | 1.5 hours | X |
| Pr26-1B | 26-2, 26-3 | Average rate of return method, net present value method, and analysis | Moderate | Analytic | Payback/ARR Methods | NPV/IRR Methods | Investment Decisions | Application | 1.5 hours | X |
| Pr26-2B | 26-2, 26-3 | Cash payback period, net present value method, and analysis | Moderate | Analytic | Payback/ARR Methods | NPV/IRR Methods | Investment Decisions | Application | 1.5 hours | X |
| Pr26-3B | 26-3 | Net present value method, present value index, and analysis | Moderate | Analytic | Payback/ARR Methods | NPV/IRR Methods | Investment Decisions | Application | 1 hour | X |
| Pr26-4B | 26-3 | Net present value method, internal rate of return method, and analysis | Moderate | Analytic | NPV/IRR Methods | | Investment Decisions | Application | 1.5 hours | |

| Problem | Learning Objective | Description | DIFFICULTY | BUSPROG Primary | ACBSP Primary | ACBSP Secondary | IMA Managerial Only | BLOOM'S | TIME | Spreadsheet |
|---|---|---|---|---|---|---|---|---|---|---|
| Pr26-5B | 26-3, 26-4 | Evaluate alternative capital investment decisions | Moderate | Analytic | NPV/IRR Methods | | Investment Decisions | Application | 1.5 hours | X |
| Pr26-6B | 26-3, 26-3, 26-5 | Capital rationing decision involving four proposals | Challenging | Analytic | Payback/ARR Methods | NPV/IRR Methods | Investment Decisions | Application | 1.5 hours | X |
| CP26-1 | 26-1 | Ethics and professional conduct in business | Easy | Ethics | NPV/IRR Methods | | Investment Decisions | Analysis | 15 min. | |
| CP26-2 | 26-2 | Personal investment analysis | Moderate | Analytic | NPV/IRR Methods | | Investment Decisions | Application | 30 min. | |
| CP26-3 | 26-3 | Changing prices | Moderate | Analytic | NPV/IRR Methods | | Investment Decisions | Analysis | 30 min. | |
| CP26-4 | 26-3 | Qualitative issues in investment analysis | Moderate | Analytic | NPV/IRR Methods | Payback/ARR Methods | Investment Decisions | Analysis | 30 min. | |
| CP26-5 | 26-2, 26-3 | Net present value method | Moderate | Analytic | NPV/IRR Methods | | Investment Decisions | Application | 30 min. | |
| CP26-6 | 26-3 | Capital investment analysis | Moderate | Analytic | NPV/IRR Methods | | Investment Decisions | Analysis | 1.5 hours | |